A NATURALIST ON RONA

AN ATLANTIC GREY SEAL BULL, RONA

A NATURALIST
ON RONA

ESSAYS OF A
BIOLOGIST IN ISOLATION

BY

F. FRASER DARLING (1903 -)

D.Sc., Ph.D., F.R.S.E.

OXFORD
AT THE CLARENDON PRESS
1939

OXFORD UNIVERSITY PRESS
AMEN HOUSE, E.C. 4
London Edinburgh Glasgow New York
Toronto Melbourne Capetown Bombay
Calcutta Madras
HUMPHREY MILFORD
PUBLISHER TO THE UNIVERSITY

FIRST PUBLISHED JUNE, 1939
REPRINTED NOVEMBER, 1939

PRINTED IN GREAT BRITAIN

PREFACE

THE web of experience is largely of your own weaving when you live on a small and remote island where there are no other human inhabitants. The little world of rock and herbage is beneath your feet and you share it with many other forms of life in which you may be interested. But only you can think reflectively, and it depends on you and your companion, if there is one, whether the island becomes a prison or a satisfying, private world for the time being. For us in our years of primitive life on three such tiny islands there has never been a dull day, though many an uncomfortable one. Our content has rested on maintaining a spirit of acceptance and having always more than enough to do—apart from goodwill within the family. I mean by a spirit of acceptance a tolerance of environmental conditions, whatever they may be, and a realization that it is no good trying to live by a routine. You must work when the work is there, and if on the next day a gale of wind and rain makes work impossible, let it be and turn your hand or mind to something else. This is the second point of having more than enough to do; I do not think anybody can be happy in the necessary restriction of island life unless there is an alternative and constructive outlet for one's energies. There has been for me on North Rona the writing of this book of essays of forest and island, in slack hours of high summer, on the impossible days of weather about the autumn equinox, and during long winter evenings when nothing could be done outside. Another man might have carved ship models or composed new airs on an accordion, but always there must be that something else to do, and more of it than can be done. Then the feet walk content within island shores, and eyes are gladdened anew each day by the march of the seasons and events in the lives of the animals which share your isolation. An island is more than a speck in the sea to a naturalist—it is usually a metropolis of the animal world and a busy port of call for a variety of migrants. The island naturalist is a gnome-like harbour-master and city chamberlain, setting everything down in his little book.

F. F. D.

NORTH RONA,
December, 1938

CONTENTS

LIST OF PLATES

I

THE VIVID FRONTIER

THERE are few natural habitats as full of dramatic interest as the sea's edge. Here is a narrow, meandering and never-ending strip of the world's surface where there are constant movement in several rhythms, a rich variety of life striving to exist and perpetuate itself, and an eternal watchfulness on the part of each individual of each species to turn some factor of the environment to its advantage. The shore is always a place of conflict and impact and reciprocation, even between the inanimate rocks and moody water; and the plants and animals of the land are for ever reaching downwards to their very limit as are those of the sea reaching out of that element to endure whatever conditions their constitutions will allow.

On and on goes this vivid strip through tropic and high latitude, through the change of seasons, and in immense variety and contrast, from the imperceptible slope of wide sands to the cliffs of remote islands and ocean frontiers. We speak sometimes of barren coasts because our mind is apt to think in terms of soil and foliage, but they are hardly ever that. To the seeing eye the stark cliffs of the north are as rich and vivid in their own way as that natural fairyland of the pools on the Great Barrier Reef of Australia.

Let me tell something of the West Highland coastline which happens to be the one with which I am most familiar. To know a coast is not merely to have an accurate memory of its shape and geographical detail, nor can a biologist with his knowledge of the ways of tiny living things know it well unless he lives by it throughout the seasons and for years. Even then, he would need to be something of a lazy fellow, one who could see farther than the platform of his microscope, and with his head not

unduly full of what passes in our modern world as education. It is my own feeling that the lobster fishermen
among the little islands know more of the sea's edge than
any one else, and though they may say very little, their
acquaintance with the sequence of lives of obscure organisms is far from superficial, nor is it unduly flavoured by
the economic aspects of their pursuits. They see, and
remember with a simple mind.

Ours is an ocean shore which bears the stress of south-
westerly gales coming from the Atlantic, but the waters
are never icy cold because the Gulf Stream wanders
north-eastwards through the maze of islands to lose itself
beyond the North Cape.

The western shore of the Outer Hebrides is of white
shell sand in many places, so the land adjoining it is green
with good grass and a place of farms. The immediate sea
is shallow and the tide-marks alter every day and at each
of the two tides. The spring tides, at the new and the full
moon, come higher and recede lower than the neap tides
which occur at the first and third quarters of the moon. In
addition to this twice-daily and twice-monthly rhythm
there is the twice-yearly one which brings the spring tides
of the spring and autumn equinoxes higher than those of
the other months. It is a flat, sandy shore which shows
these continual gradations most clearly.

The shores of the mainland and of the many small
islands are mostly rocky and of sheer cliff in many places.
Here the different zones of life appear sharply demarcated,
for the sea does not roll in over a mile of sand but over
a few yards only, or, when the cliff is sheer, the sea can
merely rise and make no invasion of the land. It is possible to sit on a rock in such a place when a spring tide is
out and see an array of the life which anchors itself to the
shore.

There are the little rock plants high up where only the
spray of great storms is driven. They are the sweet-
smelling scurvy grass which flowers earliest of all in April

PLATE I

ATLANTIC BREAKER, RONA

and continues into July; the white sea campion whose delicate sprays have none of that hard-bitten quality which is common among the plants of the cliff edge; the sea pink or thrift which colours the Highland coasts in May and June and holds a cardinal place in the human mind; there are rosettes of bucks-horn plantain and fragrant sprays of wild thyme, and sometimes in the shelter of rocks where it is not too dry the sea milkwort grows. For us who have lived on some of these tiny islands when the year has been waning, the sea milkwort has its own beauty, not so much to the sense of sight as to the smell. Those withering, golden stems crushed in the hand have the scent of autumn leaves in woods which the islands have never known.

Then comes the zone of the lichens, grey-green and golden, which cling to the face of the rocks above the spray limit of ordinary seas. Some of these composite organisms, which are the result of fungi and bacteria growing together indissolubly, provide the raw material of the vegetable dyes which the islanders use for their wool. The *cnotal* or crottal is the best known, but as part of the scenery of the sea's edge, the goat's-beard plays the larger part. How lovely is the wine-red rock of the Torridonian formation, clothed in this growth of pale green in the light of the sun!

And below the lichens are some of the plants and animals of the sea: first a narrow strip of channelled wrack on which the sheep, goats, and ponies come down to feed at low tide; then the flat wrack which makes a zone of extreme slipperiness for our feet. Next, there is a wide and diffuse strip of bladder and knotted wrack which, because of its luxuriance, provides shelter for many animals. Some of these are fixed, such as the white clusters of acorn barnacles and the red and golden masses of sea anemones; the limpets move about when the tide is over them, but they come back to rest for the dry period on particular smooth surfaces which are their very own ground and where barnacles do not get a chance to grow. The white dog-whelks and other little molluscs, such as the iridescent 'silver tommies', have a freer existence though they cling to the rock in one place while the tide is out.

The pools in this zone are thickly peopled with free-moving animals such as tiny copepods or water fleas; bull-heads, small fish of terrifying appearance with their large faces and dragon-like fins; hermit crabs with their borrowed shells scuttle away among the fronds of the wrack, and sometimes the inquisitive sticklebacks come forth to inspect our intruding fingers. They are the male fish who do this, the brilliant fellows with rosy bellies and the iris of their eyes the blue of a butterfly's wing.

Most of these plants and animals are uncovered twice each day for varying periods from one to six hours, and at their seaward limit grow the tangles, the carrageen and dulse and the thongweeds. How close is the dulse to the heart of the islander! In life it is burnished and iridescent, and when gathered it is pleasant to the taste. Many of us carry some of the dried weed to chew in moments of idleness and abstraction.

The lime-encrusted weed, *Corallina*, grows on the deep rock faces like a purple pigment laid on with an artist's palette knife. It is at this level also that the spiny globes of the sea urchins are found clinging to the cliff face and half-hidden by the waving fronds of tangle. Below that is a fairy world which we cannot truly share as the seal or the otter may, but we can gaze down into it through the clear water. Sometimes the surface is still enough to see the pulsations of those elaborate but lowly animals of radial symmetry, the jelly fish. The sea is littered with them in June; some are tiny half-globes with a purple centre, others are great yellow fellows, two feet across and with a trailing cluster of streamers. They are too refulgent to be pleasant, these exotic rays, and when we find some of them can sting the human skin, they are looked upon with even less liking. It is the warming water of the Gulf Stream which brings them about our shores.

I have mentioned the clarity of the water inshore and the beauties it allows us to see. But sometimes in May and June I have seen the water almost milky with the quantity of microscopic plankton or floating life which it holds. The minute plants of the plankton, many of which cannot be caught in the finest silk tow-nets, and are only found by centrifuging a sample of sea water, form the pastures of the sea. They are the gatherers of sunlight and the fixers of the nutritive salts of the sea. Thousands of free-swimming animals, themselves microscopic, feed on the plankton, and then a host of others, such as the copepods which we can just see with the naked eye, feed on them. Now that an appreciable size of organism in the food chain has been reached, the small fishes and crustaceans can feed. So can some of the large ones. That giant of all the fishes, the basking shark, feeds on this tiny life in the surface-layer of the sea.

That springtime milkiness denoting a superabundance of plankton soon passes. It is caused by a layer of water having come from the sea floor charged with mineral salts rich in nitrogen and phosphorus. When these are more or less exhausted the water clears again and another winter's cold and storms will be required to bring about another up-and-down movement of the water.

It is at this time of year when the northern summer is most brilliant that I like to indulge in that laziness which I have excused as being necessary to any one who would really know the continuous drama and action of the sea's edge. I like to lie on the cliff and lose the sense of hours in the grander rhythm of the sea. There is not one insignificant moment. A cloud of white birds is restless over the water; each individual is dipping and circling and screaming in the general atmosphere of excitement. They are not all birds of one species, though the general impression is whiteness. Herring gulls, kittiwakes, black-

backed and common gulls, and Arctic terns are all there,
and they are dipping to a moving shoal of coalfish. The
fish themselves may weigh many pounds each, and if we
watch their backs coming out of the water it is evident
that the gulls are not foolishly dipping at them. It is the
constant trail of excrement being made by the shoal which
attracts the birds, and they dip to it immediately before it
rapidly disintegrates and is lost to them.

The shoals of mackerel which play at the surface of the
sea have a beauty of their own, whether seen from a boat
or from the cliff. Here are many thousands of dynamic
creatures acting like one great organism. From above the
countless streamlined shapes, each one barred with that
characteristic rippling pattern, can be seen to surge forward, rise and fall, turn and turn again in a unity of movement almost unbelievable. What is the activating signal,
and what is the type of mind which can be so unified? We
have no techniques delicate enough as yet to solve these
problems and the phenomenon of the group mind must
remain a little longer a subject for wonder. When the
mackerel actually break the surface of the water the
beauty of the group action is best observed from the sea.
The sound is one of a myriad heavy raindrops in a sudden
crescendo-diminuendo of a second's duration. The sight
is one of countless spears of some invisible fairy host
waved to the raising of an unseen standard. The action is
a joyful one, and as far as I can see in the moments granted,
is caused by each fish rising nose first, forging forward,
and twisting the tail to make a tiny smack as it sounds
again.

These fish provide us with fresh food which is not to
be despised on an island where there is no garden, and
when they are taking the white fly readily I go out for them
in my kayak. Each time I pull some of them from the
water I am struck anew with their clean athletic form and
the beauty of the pattern and sheen on their skin.

The high perch on the cliff has many advantages for

watching the pageant of the sea's edge. It is not only the greater distance seen, but the ability given by such a position to see deep into the water below. The basking sharks or sail-fish are common about our shores, and when they come close in it is possible to see the slow curving movement of their progress from above. Immense and harmless fish: no one was afraid of these black, thirty-foot monsters with the shining dorsal fin showing above the water, until boats were upset by them in the Clyde. If motor-boats speed up to them and bump them or heroic gentlemen find pleasure in jabbing them with boathooks, is it surprising that one or two of them should be moved from their usual lethargic progress?

The basking sharks are common round Eilean a' Chleirich from May to August, and though as many as six have been round me while I have been fishing in my kayak, none has been 'vicious', 'treacherous', or has displayed any other of the uncomplimentary qualities attributed to it by a sensational press. It is an unfortunate habit of humanity to find still more faults in an animal once some real or imaginary one has been discovered. I have heard of owners of salmon rivers complaining that their low catches are caused by the basking sharks devouring the salmon in the sea lochs. It is difficult to make these people understand that this great fish cannot eat anything large, and that it feeds by sieving the small life of the surface-layer of the sea through its wide gill-slits.

This method of feeding by the basking sharks enables them to store large quantities of oil in their liver, which is much richer in vitamins A and D than cod-liver oil. Plankton is the richest source in the world of these vitamins, and an animal which spends so much time at the surface of the sea must be buoyant unless it is to become unduly fatigued. The basking shark, along with other and higher forms of life in the sea, such as whales and seals, develops a high content of oil under the skin and thus achieves approximately the same density as sea water.

This fish is, therefore, a natural resource of oil which might be carefully drawn upon by the coastal population each summer.

The crofter-fishermen of Barra, over a hundred years ago, had sets of tackle for harpooning the sail-fish, or *cearban* as it was called in Gaelic. Each fish yielded about eight barrels of oil. But it is recorded in that mine of information, the *New Statistical Account*, that the islanders had no tackling in 1842, when hundreds of basking sharks were to be seen. There is no reason for lessening the number of these sharks because of their being a menace to human life, but the herring fishermen have good cause for wishing them out of the way. The sail-fish blunders on his own path through herring nets as if they were not there, and the passage of a five-ton fish through these comparatively frail things almost ruins them.

There is another shark, not as large as the sail-fish, which has become much more common in the last year or two in the coastal waters of the West Highlands. It is the thrasher or fox shark, and of it we may be reasonably afraid. Without the slightest warning this fish will suddenly jump many feet from the water into the air and come down again with a terrific clap. I have seen this happen many times from my high perch on the cliff; and from there it can be viewed objectively as an imposing spectacle. But such incidents are of more immediate concern to us when we are out in the boat. The thrasher sharks are a menace when, as in 1938, we have had them jump only a few yards away from our house in the anchorage of Tanera Mor, where we are constantly going to and fro in a dinghy. These fish will attack almost anything, and a school of them will tackle a whale.

The whales are people of the deep sea and are ocean wanderers, but some of them come close inshore and even stay about the islands. Can there be a more noble sight and one more deeply stirring than to see these great mammals rise from the water? The immense nose appears first

PLATE 2

SURF: ATLANTIC GREY SEALS

and immediately the whale blows—a rapid expiration of
spent air and water vapour, and just as quick an inspiration
of fresh air. Rarely do we see that first break through the
water because we are not often looking at the exact place
where the whale rises, but the sound of his blow calls our
eyes and we see the long expanse of curved back and the
dorsal fin wheel in the water. The impression given by
this movement is that of an arc of a circle which is continued under water. His skin gleams as he goes and we
wait for the next rise. He may make three or six of these
wheel-like movements of his back above water, and each
time it is as grand as the last. I wonder if David ever saw
a whale? It is doubtful, but he had the poet's intuition
and sound imagination when he wrote those lines which,
as we know them in English, have all the grandeur and
majesty of the whale's passage through the ocean. Let me
set down again that fine piece from Psalm 104:

Oh Lord, how manifold are thy works!
In wisdom hast thou made them all;
The earth is full of thy riches.
So is the great and wide sea,
Wherein are things creeping innumerable,
Both small and great beasts.
There go the ships;
There is that leviathan, whom thou hast made to play therein.
These wait all upon thee,
That thou mayest give them their meat in due season.
That thou givest them they gather;
Thou openest thine hand, they are filled with good.[1]

For two years in succession, and at the same place, on
Eilean a' Chleirich, I saw a very large whale come directly
below me and nose about the cliff face. I saw the whole
shape of him in the water, and the gently moving flippers,
which seemed small for such an immense animal. How
little effort was needed for the propulsion of his bulk!
Sometimes I would see a school of three or four whales

[1] This excerpt is from *The Bible designed to be read as literature.*

forging through the water as fast as a ship. They would all blow at the same time, or perhaps a fraction of a second after each other. The whales move in echelon formation with absolute regularity so that the sea is broken by the four seemingly revolving arcs, each at a slightly different position of the movement. Four gleams, four sharp dorsal fins, and four oily patches on the water. The whales move on.

Some whales develop an inshore habit, and I feel justi-fied in writing of them in this essay of the sea's edge. I do not allude to those poor creatures which used to come into the Shetland voes years ago and were unable to get out when the tide ebbed. Those were occasions when whole crofting townships turned out, men and women together, to row about the voes, harpooning the whales and pulling them ashore by a stout rope tied round the tail. One day, lazing on a Shetland hill-side overlooking the western ocean, I was told a story of an old gentleman who was astride a whale's tail at the water's edge, affixing the rope. Whether he gave the whale a tweak which stimulated it to a final effort is not known, but the animal forged out into the voe with the old gentleman still aboard. He was a man of great wisdom concerning the ways of whales, said the teller of the story, for he did not try to leave his animate craft. The whale did not sound in the shallow voe and very soon it came ashore again at almost the same place where it had left. The old gentleman disembarked. That is a shining example of presence of mind, but sometimes I wish I had heard the story before it had acquired the dignity of a legend.

No, the inshore whales which come to my mind are usually young ones and they tend to develop an interest, I might almost say a friendship, for some inshore fishing-boat with its crew. My only neighbour on the island of Tanera Mor, James Macleod, points to a deep wound in the planking of his launch, which is of a double skin of teak. A few years ago a young whale used to frequent the horseshoe anchorage of the island, and when he went to the lobster creels or line-fishing in his big launch the whale would come along also, not in any cheeky or boisterous fashion, but quietly as a collie might come over the hill with you. The whale was treated decently and the friendship might be said to have been mutual. One day the whale had gone with them through the Summer Isles to the west side of Eilean a' Chleirich where the anchor was dropped. It is a bad place for an anchor, for the bottom of the sea is covered with large boulders in which the barbs are apt to get fast. The men had a good deal of twisting and turning and running astern this day before they could loosen the anchor, and then as it slowly came up they were alarmed to find that the whale had been too inquisitive and had got his tail in a loop of the anchor chain. The launch sped across the water much faster than her engine could have taken her; then all was quiet. James Macleod hauled in on the anchor again, but the whale was still on the chain. It gave a strong lashing movement with its tail against the side of the boat, and the anchor came up as if it had no weight at all. It hit the boat as well, and then the whale was free.

In pointing to that deep wound in the teak planking my neighbour suggests that a single skin of pitch pine would not have withstood the impact of the anchor barb. The poor whale was evidently as much as or more frightened than the men, for he did not come back to Tanera with the boat and, in fact, he was never seen again.

The whales and dolphins and porpoises give us only the shortest glimpses of their daily lives and we can never become intimate with them. With the seals it is different; they are nearer us in the zoological scale and they often spend hours ashore. It has been my lot to study *Ron Mor*, the great grey or Atlantic seal, more closely than most people have had time to do. He is fishing diligently during the summer months round the shores of the more remote islands, not in the lochs like his much smaller cousin, the

common seal. When *Ron Mor* raises his head my attention
is firmly held. The large eyes, shadowed by the prominent
brows, give him a look of great natural wisdom, and the
dignity is maintained by the strength of his profile. Up
comes the shining head from the waves, the nostrils dilate
while he takes deep breaths, and down he goes again with a
roll in less than a minute, his lungs replenished. He is
out of sight then for five or seven minutes while he fishes.

The drama of the sea's edge which I mentioned in my
opening sentence is evident in one of its most spectacular
forms when a huge surf is beating against the cliffs of one
of the seal islands. It is common to read such an expression as 'nothing could live in that terrible surf'. So it
seems, looking down into the turmoil and hearing the
continual roar. But the great seals seek it as a playground.
They impart a joyousness to the scene as their gleaming
forms bob out of the foam, or stand in the wall of a
breaker which may be twice as high as they are long, and
dive below its shattering crest. Yearlings, cows, and adult
bulls, they are all there enjoying the fun. The sea's edge,
which is still a necessity to the seals at the breeding
season, is a place of conflict and danger for them at that
time, but for all the rest of the year the seal is master of
his element, and I believe he knows it.

The sea otters add to the constant interest of the shore
on Eilean a' Chleirich. This island is an otter's paradise
with its freshwater lochs close to the sea and the abundance
of caves and cairns among the boulders. There must be
a population of twenty or thirty of them on an island of
three hundred acres. We saw much more of the otters in
the second year of our life there, and we have wondered if
they had learned to accept us as harmless human beings.
Mothers and youngsters ran along the lochan's edge and
pairs of them were commonly seen playing in the sea
beneath the cliffs. Is there any more playful animal than
this one? Whenever there are two together, all seriousness seems to pass away and they wrestle and play hide-

and-seek. Fishing is good at night time, and when I have been out of a calm night in the kayak when it was almost dark, I have occasionally heard a tiny and pleasing sound, and I have let the paddle rest. It has been the sharp and regular sibilance of an otter's breathing as he has swum near me with just his nostrils and eyes above water. Once the small round head came near enough for me to see the wondering eyes. The darkness on the sea on a good night is far from absolute and I saw a face I might have missed in the light of day.

The bird life of the shore adds in large measure to the ceaseless activity and change which the human observer feels to be taking place. If we go through the British List of birds it is striking to find how many of them have either temporary or permanent association with the sea's edge. Some birds, like the raven, peregrine falcon, and buzzard live at the cliff edges because man has driven them there; they are as fugitives at the edge of the land. Others come to feed at the shore in season, such as the purple sandpiper, the dunlin, the curlew, and the heron; and some find their whole lives occupied in this zone, as do the rock pipit, turnstone, and oyster catcher.

The shag is a bird of the shallow sea, but it spends much of its time on the rocks in the company of its fellows. Its beautiful under-water action of closed wings and the powerful feet thrusting back the water in unison is well seen from above. Even as I write these lines on the cliff edge of North Rona there is some brilliant fishing going on below me. By wearing Polaroid spectacles and gazing through my binoculars I can see an immense shoal of small eels wriggling in the sea. They seem to be moving all the time and getting nowhere. A shag has dived and with lightning movements hither and thither and up and down he is snapping up the eels. What is a score or two of individuals from the shoal? The multitude continues to wriggle indifferently. The shag comes up and shakes the jewel-like drops from the burnished green of his back.

I am not justified in saying he is pleased, but he looks it all the same.

There is another large group of birds which come to the cliffs only at the breeding season, and for them the shore is the edge of the sea. They are the auk tribe—the puffin, razorbill, and guillemot; the kittiwake gulls, and those members of another ocean-going family—the fulmar petrel, the Manx shearwater and the tiny swallow-like storm petrel. Here on Rona and on those other remote islands of our country, the Flannans and St. Kilda, there is also to be witnessed the exciting aerial dance in the night time of Leach's fork-tailed petrel.

All these birds have their small but cumulative effect on the other flora and fauna of the coast. I have found the weeds of arable land growing in the sea cliffs of lonely islands; these have come as seeds in the crops of gulls foraging on the mainland when the corn is sown. The droppings and the fish offal also help to manure the region of the cliffs so that its flora is different from that only a few yards farther inland, and consequently the soil fauna is different as well.

A cliff of sea birds in early summer is indeed the vivid frontier. Birds are essentially creatures of emotion, and as the human being is also possessed of a more emotional nature than many other animals, it is impossible for a human observer to remain indifferent to the surge of joy in living which is apparent in such a vast concourse of birds. The postures of display and their significance are the subject of another essay in this book, but in this place let us see the cliff and its teeming population with the eye of the artist.

Consider the colour scheme presented by a colony of kittiwakes against one of the cliffs which faces the east anchorage of Rona. It is early morning when the cliff is sunlit and I go there to watch and to take photographs. The dominant colours in this natural arrangement are grey and green, supplemented by white. There is nothing

PLATE 3

TRESHNISH ISLES: THE DUTCHMAN FROM LUNGA

garish. The dull grey of the Hebridean Gneiss is the background and growing from it, where a modicum of earth
has managed to lodge, is a wealth of scurvy grass. This
plant is not a grass at all, but an annual of flat, shiny leaves
of a green which is not bright, and a stem of small white
flowers comes from the centre of each mass. Here and
there on the rock where the water has dripped and drained
continuously there are streaks of a quiet, deep green made
by growths of algae. The kittiwakes have made little
shallow platforms of nests on seemingly impossible ledges,
and the nests and round about them have become soiled
with white excrement. Then there are the birds themselves with their pure white heads and breasts, and
mantles of the most delicate silver grey. The background
is lovely in itself but the birds are never still against it.
They are the most expressive of the gulls with which I am
familiar, and this scene, composed of a quiet scheme of
colours, throbs with an urgent, vivid life. The crying of
the birds is a tumult, and though each individual cry is
discordant, the whole is a sound of exciting beauty.

The guillemots breed on the ledges in close masses very
near to the kittiwakes. Their activity is almost ecstatic.
The sharp black and white of their plumage does not
break harshly on the restful colouring of the background
I have described. Their skirling cries join in the grand
symphony of the bird cliff.

The puffin towns are placed on the grassy tops of the
cliffs or on steep slopes where these birds can dig long
burrows in which to nest. Here is a different colour
scheme. The grass is a brilliant green, their plumage is a
sharp black and white offset by legs of orange-red, a grey
face, and a large multi-coloured beak in which orange-red
and yellow predominate. A gathering of puffins on the
green is like that of a gay and distinguished garden party.
But the deportment of each individual puffin is not gay
or abandoned, apart from the frequent flapping of their
wings. The puffin's mien is solemn, or it would be more

scientifically accurate to say expressionless, and he is not given to noisy ebullitions of emotion. His voice is a long-drawn-out croak of some dignity, uttered in the depths of his burrow.

The hosts of these birds I have mentioned are constantly flying forth from the cliffs of the islands where they breed and crossing the frontier of the sea's edge. Sometimes they go for food, sometimes in fright, and often enough for nothing at all but the short fly out and back again. The activity is incessant and overwhelming. Even as I write these lines, sitting in my neuk in the cliff of Rona, the peregrine falcon has dashed by, uttering her harsh, grating bark. This dread sound sends thousands of puffins flying from the cliff, and from so many small lives the falcon takes her toll in a fatal stoop. It seems strange that the puffins should not have learnt to stay on the cliff when the peregrine passes by, for she only takes her prey in flight. But no, the whole cliff of birds is in a panic and the little puffins who, after all, seem to have more beak than brain, pay the price. They never fight back and they do not complain. They are anybody's meat, as it were, and the whole race, expressed in the quiet eye of each individual, seems to have accepted a philosophy of resignation or indifference to this fate.

Indeed, this is the lesson and the story of the sea's edge. Life teems and dies that life may continue. There is a burgeoning and an exuberance in most of the forms of life, and through the intricacy and wholeness of the pattern the masses of the species are sieved at every step. The vivid frontier is a place of many rhythms, of impact, conflict, and reciprocation. On and on it goes, a never-ending strip, through tropic and high latitude.

II

THE DISPLAY OF BIRDS

THE behaviour of birds fascinates a very large number of people who would call themselves neither biologists nor naturalists. I remember a gentleman whose subject was not science describing to me, during dinner, an accurate series of experiments which he conducted in his garden, and from which he found that the boundary line between the territories of two robins was about eighteen inches wide. His work had taken time and that patience of a high order which the calm of a university city engenders. I also remember a London business man whose offices were in a block of high flats. He had a good many interesting observations to make on the heights above ground most favoured by the common birds of London.

The grace of form and flight, the quickness and lightness of movement, and the rich variety of bird life which shares the immediate neighbourhood of human activities, all make for an interest which is constant, though possibly superficial. But there is also the provoking riddle of the bird's mind. Few creatures, we reflect, are more ready to take advantage of any change in the environment which happens to suit them, and yet they seem bound in the most rigid fashion by what we call instinct. The riddle is there, and it exercises the don and the stockbrocker as much as the biologist.

The phenomenon of display in the life of birds, which usually appears at the breeding season, is one of the most exciting aspects of avian behaviour. The problem it offers is in part solved, and the history of the research which has been done on the subject is a good example of the fruitful co-operation of field naturalists with physiologists and psychologists. And, happily, the story is not yet complete; most subjects of inquiry are the better for a little remaining mystery.

The contrariness by human standards which is seen in the behaviour of birds may be better understood if the radical difference between the avian and mammalian brain is kept in mind. The evolution of the bird's brain has been marked by the development in size and complication of the corpus striatum; in no other group does this portion of the brain affect overt behaviour to such an extent. This development has meant that the bird has a very large endowment of inherited instinct or unlearned ability to live. The cerebral cortex, which is present in all brains above the amphibian, still remains as a very thin and un-developed layer in the avian brain. It is the growth and elaboration of the cortex which characterizes the mammalian brain, and this layer of grey matter enables the mammal to cope with situations as problems, with varying degrees of clearness. The cortex is most fully developed in man, and together with our thumbed hand and upright carriage it has made us human. The mammal has a more ready capacity for learning and for intelligent adaptation to circumstances; the bird, on the other hand, endowed so richly with stock reactions to situations, has in some measure to unlearn before it can adapt its behaviour to new problems. Conjecture on the future development of avian behaviour would lead us to the idea of further perfection of instinctive reaction, coupled with delicate thresholds of emotion in which the companion or the community in which the bird lives would play a large part.

Display is an expression of instinctive emotion concerned with reproduction, and to a lesser extent with anger. I do not propose to deal with anger in this essay, but it is worth keeping in mind that anger is on the verge of much of the behaviour appearing in the whole reproductive cycle of animals, more particularly of the males. And in many birds it is the male which plays the most prominent part in display. The physiological processes

leading up to reproduction undoubtedly influence behaviour, but there is a reciprocative effect as well, for the
display of birds helps towards the maturation and synchronization of the reproductive state between the sexes.

Darwin watched birds displaying with very great
interest and wrote on the subject in many of his works,
particularly in *The Descent of Man*. He put forward the
theory of sexual selection in birds, based on the conclusion
that display was an activity which allowed the female to
choose her mate, and by this means brilliant plumage and
intricate display patterns would be evolved. This theory
is open to many objections, but it was not until this century that a more constructive one was offered. We owe
our present knowledge primarily to Mr. Eliot Howard.

His monograph on the British warblers, published
between 1908 and 1914, showed the importance of song in
the delimitation of the breeding territories of these birds.
His own patient observations showed that the males
migrate first to the country where breeding takes place,
and that song is an advertisement of the male's presence
in a given area. The females follow after a week or ten
days, and their reproductive condition is far behind that of
the males. When the hen bird has elected to stay inside
the territory of a cock, she has to learn the boundaries, and
though she may be amenable to the attentions of the male,
she is far from being in a ready condition to mate with
him physically. For all general purposes it can be said
that the male bird has an asexual and a sexual phase fairly
sharply defined. The female has an intermediate, slowly
ripening phase, and it is at this time that the display postures indulged in by the cock have the greatest significance
or valency for her. The visual pattern of his movements
affect her physiologically and in due time the two birds
are ready to pair.

This synchronization of pairing condition is a subject
which Mr. Howard developed more fully in his later books,
Territory in Bird Life, and especially in *An Introduction to*

the Study of Bird Behaviour, 1929, and it is since then that physiologists have been able to demonstrate the processes within the body by which visual patterns can affect the state of the reproductive organs.

Dr. F. H. A. Marshall of Cambridge, in his Croonian Lecture of 1936 to the Royal Society of London, showed the evolutionary value of display to be the more effective synchronization of the pairing condition. If it should be asked why this moment should be of greater importance in birds than in many other animals, it should be remembered that the sexual act in birds is a difficult feat to accomplish, and that unless both birds were in equally ardent condition it could not take place at all. Dr. Marshall concluded that 'those birds which have brighter colours, more elaborate ornamentation, and a greater power of display must be supposed to possess a superior capacity for effecting . . . a close degree of physiological adjustment between the two sexes'. The sexually selective value of display, adornment, and the development of the aesthetic sense is therefore none the less real, but Dr. Marshall's interpretation does not carry with it the objections which did Darwin's supposition of preferential choice by the female.

There are four broad types of display in what we somewhat erroneously call the courtship behaviour of birds, and the phenomenon is better understood as a whole if the differentiation is clear in our minds. First, there is the type common among the song birds. Here we find that the plumages of the two sexes are not very markedly different, nothing more striking than between a cock and hen bullfinch, and usually much less than that in songsters of the quality of warblers, thrushes, robins, and wrens.

To take the warblers as an example, the first part of the reproductive phase in the males is not concerned with reproduction at all. That energy is canalized in the first place to migration, to the activities of advertisement and defiance by singing from some high vantage point, and

PLATE 4

A COMMON GUILLEMOT AND HER BRIDLED MATE: RONA

THE DISPLAY OF BIRDS

then to the delimitation of a territory. All this is in progress before the females appear, and when they do come their choice of a male is nothing more than settling into a territory owned by one cock. Indeed, two hen warblers arriving simultaneously at the territory of a cock bird may fight for possession of him, or perhaps it would be more correct to say they fight to stay in that place, and as the warblers are monogamous during the rearing of each brood, one of them must go. The male warbler watches these encounters passively.

It is known that such pairings are frequently not constant beyond the rearing of one brood. If a hen bird then elects to change her immediate district, the cock will assert no overlordship beyond the boundaries of his own territory. The later phase of the reproductive period of the male is given up in part to encouragement of the female by various display postures. These may be ardent and intense but rarely elaborate, and they are not supported by any extraordinary bright colourings. The display responses of the female are weak or non-existent. She may do little more than eventually place herself in a position for coition to take place.

Secondly, there is the type of display between members of a pair which is mutual and reciprocative. This may occur in birds which are similar in plumage and not extraordinarily brilliant of colouring, or there may be well-defined differences and obvious ornamentation in the male. The delimitation of territory may be confined to that immediately surrounding the nest and not including a large and private food territory as in the warblers. This applies particularly where such birds are social at the breeding season and they are common in this group. The patterns vary in their elaborateness and in the degree of ecstasy reached, but the common feature is that the display is reciprocative, essentially so. One action by the male, who most commonly initiates a period of display, is followed by a responsive action by the female, which in turn excites the cock to a further stage of the complicated pattern. The pigeon, the shag, and the grebe come within this group.

Thirdly, there is a communal type of display. It may be taking place between the members of pairs within the flock all at the same time. It may be in the nature of a set piece between all the birds in the flock without essential reference to pairs, or the whole flock may indulge in an apparently random bout of activity to which we are unable to assign a pattern. It is common to find that there is no difference in plumage between males and females of birds acting in this way, though their plumage patterns may, nevertheless, be striking. The display of many sea birds falls into this section of my rough classification, and the species may be as far apart as the gulls from the guillemots. Herons, which normally nest in colonies, have a communal dance of grace and charm, and the magpie is a bird of the land which has a marked tendency to communal display at the opening of the breeding season, though it may not nest in a flock. The display of members of the petrel family can also be included in this section.

Fourthly, there is that highest pitch of display in which the male only takes part, and in our British birds such display is communal, though in an entirely different way from that of the third type. Here the males gather at some place well known to them and go through a series of display patterns of excessive punctilio and elaborateness. The bodily postures and movements are enhanced in effect by brilliant colourings and ornamentations of the plumage. In some species, such as the great bustard, the feathers of the neck are raised to exhibit brightly coloured patches of skin as well. Birds which indulge in this highly formalized type of display are the black grouse, its near cousin the capercailzie, and that little wading bird, the ruff. In each case the female is passive as far as participation in the display is concerned, but there is no doubt that she sees what is happening and certain males are more successful in coition afterwards than others.

This most advanced type of display practised by highly ornamented males is found to occur in species which are naturally promiscuous or at least polygamous. The females are of extremely sober colouring and enjoy the protection which it gives during the period of incubating the eggs and rearing the chicks. The males take no part whatever in parental duties and this phenomenon is carried to its limit in the breeding of the ruff and reeve. The males collect at a 'hill' well known to them. They spar about the well-trodden area indulging in formalized fighting which causes them no damage; and in a state of ecstasy the birds squat, beak forward, wings outstretched and, quite naturally, the gaily-coloured ruff of feathers fully visible. Such females as occasionally collect at the 'hill' may then come forward and lightly touch the males of their choice with their bill. Mating takes place and the sexes part. The males are presumably unaware of the nesting-places taken up by the reeves.

I have come to the conclusion that in such birds as the blackcock and ruff, where display is essentially a gathering and an activity of males, successful breeding is accomplished only when it is possible for such displays to take place. The ruff is no longer a species breeding in Britain, though the birds frequently appear in some of the Norfolk sanctuaries where ample protection would be given them. If a dozen ruffs appeared instead of ones and twos, there would be a good chance of display developing as, for example, it does in the London Zoo where conditions are far from being ideal. Black game have decreased very markedly in recent years despite general efforts to maintain numbers by owners of moors. It is said that the primary cause of the decline was an epidemic of coccidiosis; but it is the way of populations of animals to recover from epidemics, and not to be reduced by them to the verge of extinction. Occasional non-breeding pairs of black game are found on some moors where they were formerly plentiful, and if my conclusion is correct they remain nonbreeders because there are not sufficient males to gather together for display at a *lek*,[1] by which means they would attain to the final pitch of preparedness for mating. It should be remembered that the blackcock's close cousin, the capercailzie, became extinct in the eighteenth century, though as a game bird it would be given such protection as was possible. After its reintroduction in 1837 it became fairly numerous once more in eastern Scotland. Those who have watched the species have found that in the course of its diffusion it is the females which colonize first, and they may breed with blackcock until a sufficient number of males of their own kind are in the neighbourhood. As the capercailzie is also a species in which the males display socially, there would be little good in single males attempting to colonize.

The examples of the ruff and black game are the extreme. Let us consider the display of some of the birds I have mentioned earlier and the place it takes in their family lives.

Those warblers and less brightly coloured small birds to which I first called attention have display patterns which are not very elaborate. The wings may be drooped and spread or rapidly vibrated and the throat feathers puffed out. The males continue to sing throughout this period. The pipits make small soaring flights and volplane steeply with a descending note of song. All these small birds desperately need the protection of their comparatively dull colours, for they are the prey of hawks and small carnivores. The small song birds are also wholly insectivorous at the breeding and rearing season, and this habit of feeding means an almost ceaseless search to provide for a large nestful of youngsters. The hen could certainly not do it alone and the male works equally hard. The warblers could not possibly have survived as a race had the males developed a bright and metabolically expensive plumage

---

[1] *Lek* is the name given to the traditional places where blackcock gather for display.

which, as I think, would have precluded their taking an active part in the immense task of food gathering for helpless young birds.

As an example of the second type of display I might cite the courtship behaviour of the great crested grebe which was the subject of one of Dr. Julian Huxley's early scientific papers. It is a bird which I have not had the opportunity as yet of watching closely myself. The birds go through a ritual of exciting movements which draws forth responses from one and the other. They face each other and shake their heads violently; the male dives and rises from the water extremely slowly—first the head with ruff extended and beak downwards. Then he slowly rises to his full height, standing upright in the water. A further display involves the gathering of a morsel of weed by each member of the pair. They come above water several yards from each other and dash almost together at great speed. They do not quite meet but rise up to their full height, beaks pointing together with the weed between them. They sway in an ecstasy for a few moments.

The remarkable seasonal head-dress is undoubtedly exciting to the mate and the display is not confined to the period just before nidification and egg-laying. It continues until the young are well grown, and Dr. Huxley's opinion is that as the male helps in incubation and food gathering for the young, the display which so obviously gives pleasure to both partners serves as an emotional bond of a union in which protraction till late in the season has a definite biological value.

I have seen less elaborate display in the shag continuing far through the breeding season. This bird of the cliff and shallow sea lives a life comparable with that of the grebe on fresh water. The plumage is burnished black-green and a recurved black crest is grown just before the onset of the breeding time. Each bird strokes the head and neck of the other with its bill, and after a few moments they extend their necks and beaks upwards as far as possible and remain in this rapt attitude for several seconds. I confess that this long-continued type of display between members of a pair gives me the greatest pleasure to watch. The mutual joy of graceful movement in birds which share their parental duties brings them for the moment nearer to our own ideal, an ideal of a golden age which we never seem to reach.

Gulls display in many ways, both as individuals of a pair and as a flock. But their actions do not reach the highly formalized pitch of that found in the grebe. The plumage of gulls would not be called brilliant, but it is striking in its sharp whiteness against the background of the gullery and, as is suggested in another essay, the effect of movement and display within the flock may have a cumulative value for the individuals throughout. Display is sporadic, a matter of a few seconds' duration, but varied and frequent.

From my own work on black-backed and herring gulls I have found at least ten actions which I could interpret as display. The early stages of the breeding cycle are marked by the birds lowering their heads, arching their necks, and uttering a long, wailing cry. The head may be lowered suddenly and the neck so steeply arched that the head is almost inverted for a moment between the legs. The head is then thrown upwards to the fullest extent and a loud cry of many syllables comes from the widely opened beak.

These are early patterns and vociferous ones, and are infectious in character, but later the display patterns take place most commonly in the small area of the nesting territory, and they are quieter. There is, nevertheless, a vocal pattern distinctive of nearly all the visual patterns of display. When I used to spend nights in my hide at the gullery, I would wake in the grey of the morning and before raising myself to look through the peep-hole, I would listen awhile to the sounds outside. I could tell what was happening quite easily by these distinctive cries.

I found that in gulls many of the more intimate display patterns were in the nature of a pretence or shadow-show of events to come. The pairs would act the procedure of changing shifts in incubating the eggs and of brooding them, long before eggs were there at all. Then they would play the part of mock-feeding, male to female, an action which becomes real when the hen bird is taking her long spells of incubation. And finally, there is a pattern of mock-coition which is certainly not attempted coition. It would seem that acting the coming stages in the breeding cycle has a definite effect in furthering its course—and after all, that is what we should expect.

Sometimes gulls indulge in communal display which I should still include in my third type, although the birds do not appear to follow a set pattern or ritual such as I shall shortly describe as taking place in such birds as the black guillemot and the razorbill. The gulls would make sudden and silent up-flights of a few seconds' duration above the gullery; the black-backed gulls would soar as a flock very high into the air. Up and up they go until they look small in the sky; then they whirl round and round and across and across in ways the human eye cannot follow. Their descent is effortless, marked by dips and spins and occasional short 'zooms' upward again. The waxing and waning of intense excitement, and the blue sky of early summer patterned by the wheeling birds, provides an experience of rhapsodic pleasure to the human observer anchored to the ground below. I think we can hardly doubt that a large part of the charm of birds for humanity lies in the fact that we and they find similar things beautiful—patterns and displays of colour and grace of movement.

And now to describe some of those communal forms of display of the third type in my arbitrary grouping: their value lies not only in their power to synchronize the breeding condition of each pair, but to raise the threshold of reproductive activity throughout the flock.

Consider the beauty of a flock of black guillemots or tysties. Their plumage is jet black, relieved by a large and sharply outlined patch of white on the wings. The feet are vermilion red, and almost the same colour appears again inside their beaks, which they are constantly opening to utter a plaintive and high-pitched 'peeeeee'. Here is a combination of colours initially striking enough, but when the communal pattern of display is in progress the effect is kaleidoscopic. Small groups of from four to twelve gather on the surface of the sea and play of an infectious kind begins. They duck, they dive, they rise out of the water and flap their wings; all sink an inch or two below the surface and swim about and in and out in a complex figure. There may follow then a more formal dance. The group forms a rank and swims closely in line; they turn and come back again; then a half turn, so that the birds move in echelon for a time; or perhaps another half turn will bring them into single file. The springtime dances on the sea occur so often and in such orderly fashion that it is impossible to set them down as random formations.

Here is another dance I have seen among razorbills, and I will quote the description from my book *Bird Flocks and the Breeding Cycle*:

'The birds were almost in single file at first, and because their legs cannot be seen moving beneath the water, it seemed as if the movement of the sea itself brought the birds into a group, beaks inward. Their raised beaks almost touched in the centre; the circle enlarged and broke; each pair of birds bobbed and both members came together and held beaks. In this fashion the pairs waltzed round for a few seconds. Then all the birds formed into single file again, headed in one direction, and struck a posture of ecstasy which was maintained for three or four seconds. The beaks were lifted high and slightly open and the tails were raised even higher than normally. The ring and the pairs were formed again, and the state of ecstasy was reached while the members of the pairs were facing each other; then more waltzing and the curious single file and the posture of rapture throughout the flock once more. The whole display lasted for about a quarter of an hour,

PLATE 5

PUFFINS, RONA: ONE WITH A BEAKFUL OF SMALL FISH

after which the birds began the common occupation of wing-flapping and preening, and finally they rose from the water and flew seawards, just topping the waves.'

The phenomenon of display is often bound up in subtle fashion with that of nest-building, at least in those species which make any semblance of a nest at all. And it is the male which initiates this work, providing the link between his display and the serious task of the female in building a workman-like nest. Warblers and buntings sometimes build several rough nests and the activity seems to be an outlet for surplus energy as well as one suggestive and exciting to the female. The reader may be referred to the vivid descriptions of the courtship of these birds in Mr. Eliot Howard's books mentioned earlier.

Once the female is embarked upon building her nest, the presentation to her of nesting material appears to arouse her pleasurable feelings, and in many instances this giving and receiving partakes of the character of display. Sometimes, indeed, the objects and material given by the male bird have no constructional value in nest-building, but they are in the nature of ornaments and therefore acceptable. No description can adequately convey the tenderness with which the male herring gull and black-backed gull, birds far from tender in most aspects of their lives, will pluck a flower of sea pink and lay it before the female at the nest. These birds also seek pretty shells and bleached fragments of bone to lay before their mate so that the nest and its immediate neighbourhood becomes littered with a collection which would rival the contents of small boys' pockets. I have known the birds carry pieces of paper and lemon peel from our camp to decorate their nests, and occasionally they have pulled up my little wooden garden labels for the same purpose when I had been using them at the gullery for identifying certain nests and recording data.

Those little birds the tysties which we watched at their communal dance of display do not nest in groups, but singly in crevices of the cliffs and among the boulders. The male brings to his mate small, flat pebbles or flakes of rock which she disposes into the form of a surprisingly flat and comfortable nest like a saucer. The pebbles now so prettily set may have a purpose in keeping the eggs together, but in view of the places in which the eggs are laid, it is more likely that the first value of the stones was as an intermediary of private display between the pair. And those little flakes of rock of just the right size are not so common that the little bird does not need to put considerable industry into the task of finding them. Of our northern auks the tysties are the only ones which give and receive stones at the breeding-season, but among their cousins the penguins of the southern hemisphere the practice seems to be taken to an extreme and rather ridiculous limit. Commander Murray Levick in his books on the life of Antarctic penguins describes the perpetual farce of gathering and stealing stones, and the presentation of them with a bow at the feet of the females.

It is natural that birds should display in a manner which shows and exercises the activities at which they are most adept, and we are thus able to see more wonderful exhibitions of such inherent skill than we might in the ordinary, everyday life of the birds. Consider, for example, the aerobatics of the ravens in February and March; the exciting twirls and somersaultings carry flight to a greater complexity than is usually necessary. But it is not unreasonable to believe that such practice may have a value in later emergency, and we can go even farther and say that the superlative displays of skill at these times have an evolutionary value beyond that of their significance at the breeding-season. The diving display of grebes and the incredibly swift mock-stooping and zooming of the peregrine falcon before his mate are in the same class of inherently useful activity. But all display is beautiful, and its appeal through the aesthetic sense of birds on the reproductive organs by way of the anterior pituitary gland is one of the wonderful manifestations of nature which we have but lately come to understand. The appeal to our own sense of beauty is very strong and may in no small part urge us forward to closer watching and fuller interpretation.

It is a habit of the pundits of the scientific world to discourage the representation of the facts of science in other than coldly objective description, often with the use of a technical phraseology which is little more than jargon. The aim of science should certainly be to remove the mystery from natural phenomena, but not to take away wonder or that quality of nature which allows for the development and play of aesthetic appreciation. The objective analysis of nature is a field from which the artistic mind may gather strength and stimulation, to recreate from and interpret what is learned there. The deterministic attitude is, perhaps, a reaction from the type of representation which adorns facts or waters them down for a public not greatly interested.

The display of birds can be almost fully explained in terms of hormones, motor-mechanisms, stimuli, and responses. I say almost, because such a method neglects the wholeness of the bird's existence and it attempts to neglect, or professes itself unconcerned with, the very real set of impressions made on the mind of the beholder. Let the plain facts of scientific analysis be made known, but let them also be synthesized again for a fuller and more enlightened artistic appreciation which will blend them the better into the richness of our experience.

III

NORTH RONA

O these endless little isles! and of all little isles this Ronay! Yet,
much as hath been seen, not to see thee, lying clad with soft verdure,
and in thine awful solitude, afar off in the lap of wild ocean,—not to
see thee with the carnal eye, will be to have seen nothing!

THESE lines were written over eighty years ago by the
Scots ecclesiastical archaeologist, T. S. Muir, after his
visit to North Rona when he measured and drew the ruins
of St. Ronan's cell and the ancient chapel. The lines show
none of the ornate style of the age in which they were
drafted; they are clear as the sunshine of Rona, and the
little island shines through them bright to the reader's
mind. More than three hundred years before Muir, Rona
received its first written mention from the High Dean of
the Isles, Sir Donald Monro, in his famous manuscript of
1549. His reference is short, but I think these words have
a right sense in them and are fitting: '. . . ane little ile callit
Ronay, . . . inhabit and manurit[1] be simple people . . .'

The 'little ile callit Ronay' remains green and fresh; the
simple people have gone, being starved to death in the
seventeenth century. I feel this tragedy deeply, because
not only a culture but a race died as well. Dean Monro
said they were 'scant of ony religione'; Martin Martin
shows them to have been very religious in the seventeenth
century when he cites the Presbyterian minister of Barvas
in Lewis, who visited Rona in the last years of the people's
existence. The minister was evidently sternly calvinistic
and was not pleased when one of the men, after a beauti-
fully worded welcome,

'would needs express his high esteem for my person, by making
a turn round about me sun-ways, and at the same time blessing me,
and wishing me all happiness; but I bid him let alone that piece of

---

[1] *Manurit*—in the archaic sense—worked.

PLATE 6

THE WEST CLIFF OF RONA

homage, telling him I was sensible of his good meaning towards me: but this poor man was not a little disappointed, as were also his neighbours; for they doubted not but this ancient ceremony would have been very acceptable to me; and one of them told me, that this was a thing due to my character from them, as to their chief and patron, and they could not, nor would not fail to perform it.'

Poor, ignorant minister! His religion had destroyed his tact. The simple people rose above this rebuff, for in addition to giving him refreshment and a bed of clean straw, each household, five in all, killed a sheep and skinned it whole from head to tail, so that the pelt could be used as a sack. The skins were filled with barley meal and given to the minister as a present. Five skinfuls of meal was a present of no mean order from a population of thirty souls, getting their whole subsistence from a bare Atlantic island of three hundred acres, of which only a few were ploughed.

It was a few years after this that a plague of rats came ashore from a ship and ate up the whole sustenance of the island. And in the space of a few months some seamen landed and stole the island bull. 'The steward of St. Kilda being by a storm driven in there, told me [Martin Martin] that he found a woman with a child on her breast, both lying dead at the side of a rock.' So died these simple people who took their surnames 'from the colour of the sky, rain-bow and clouds'. The rats have also gone; if these animals are to subsist on an island they must have a safe shore stocked with shell-fish.

Martin records that the people had the second sight and that they received apparitions of visitors before their arrival. It is the way of the islands. Long periods of island life under simple and lonely conditions have made me depend more on intuition than the man of science in me has been prepared to approve. North Rona has affected me in this way more than anywhere else, and without any attempt at justification or explanation, and in the face of

possible ridicule, I say that during my months on Rona I
have had knowledge and have spoken of coming events
with an accuracy and clarity which have been disturbing.
Reason, that cold reason which I do not trust, but to which
I must tender lip-service at least because it governs my
scientific work, says one thing; my intuition says another
in the face of gathering facts and indications; and my
intuition does not fail me. Sometimes the truth comes in
sleep, sometimes when I am wide awake, and as I say,
the regularity of its coming on Rona has disturbed me. I
will not attempt description because I have no interest in
explaining or taking sides one way or the other. I experience; I record.

The people have gone but their works remain. Nothing
on Rona makes me remember them more poignantly than
the few acres of lazy beds[1] where they grew their barley and
oats. These patches of ground, once cultivated and now
growing a good turf rich with the fragrance of white clover
in July, are more appealing than the strange dwellings of
the ruined village above the lazy beds on the southern
slope. A low sun from the west gives each ridge of good
earth a shadow which falls in the hollows, and the pattern
of the several strips is clear. There is a touch of pathos also
in the two quern stones, perfect but for the wooden
handle, which are lying on one of the dykes among the
ruins.

The dyke surrounding the cultivated ground is only one
or two stones high, and as it is hardly credible that any one
has since carried stones away from this boundary, I think
the fence cannot have been any more formidable than it is
now, unless it was made up with driftwood, of which
there seems to have been a plentiful supply in earlier days,
when ships were made of wood. Small island communi-

---

[1] Lazy-bed cultivation is common in the West Highlands and west of
Ireland and refers to the practice of banking the soil in low ridges of
about three yards across and following the slope of the ground. The soil
of the ridges is dry and the hollows form the natural drainage channels.

ties often tether their cattle and sheep, and this may
have been the method followed on Rona. There would be
no school for the children and they would be available as
well in helping to keep the animals from the cultivated
ground in spring and summer.

Dykes of stone and turf of considerable strength are
found round the old dwellings and the best example is that
round the chapel and burial ground. It is eight feet thick
and four feet high at present and is built in a beautiful,
regular curve. The houses themselves are half under-
ground and in the time of their occupation the earth was
doubtless banked up to the eaves. But now the earth has
fallen away from some of them and the stone skeleton is
left. Soon they will fall in and be mere rickles of stones
like the Teampull nam Manach which was once standing
a few yards east of Ronan's cell.[1]

The entrances to the houses were low tunnels along
which the people must have gone on hands and knees.
Tunnels also lie alongside the main room of the two
houses best preserved and it is difficult fully to understand
the architecture and economy of the dwellings. The
passages were roofed by long slabs of stone placed transversely, and it is still evident that at least part of the roof
of the houses themselves was of these long slabs of stone,
each course extending inwards a little beyond the last.
We know from Martin Martin, nevertheless, that the
final roof-covering was straw, kept down by ropes of
straw on which boulders were suspended in the well-
known way of the Isles.

These houses are probably of very great age and they
would persist as habitations in the style they are because
of the isolation of the community on Rona and because of

---

[1] This allusion to a temple built and demolished is taken from *Ronay*
by Malcolm Stewart, Oxford University Press, 1933. Mr. Stewart has
summarized the recorded history of North Rona and has detailed his
sources, so I shall try not to go over the ground covered by him except in
so far as I have my own comments to add.

the limitations of material available to the islanders. It is difficult to understand why this unique village site has not been cared for adequately by the State. It is a relic of the Stone Age which has been inhabited well into historical times. There are other relics of a Stone-Age culture on Rona, not contemporary with the Megalithic period but a relic of its culture all the same. These are the beehive shielings which remain on the stark northern peninsula of Fianuis and the one on Sceapull. I believe they are of comparatively recent construction, built as shelters for the sealers from Ness who made the journey each year in November. The seals are mostly to be found on Fianuis, and though November is getting on towards the end of the breeding-season, it is a time of year when there is usually a calm and settled spell, suitable for the journey from Ness in the open boat which the sealers used.

One of these shielings is in a fairly good state of preservation, and we ourselves have repaired it and cleaned out the floor, so that it could be used as an emergency lodge if the huts blew down. The inside is about fourteen feet long and eight feet wide, and the corners are rounded to make the shape more or less oval. Entrance is by an open doorway two and a half feet high in the eastern end, outside which is a passage-way with a double twist in it to baffle the wind. The height of the inside wall is about six feet, at which level there has been already a distinct thrust inwards all round. As I have looked at the place, I think the men who built and used it must have done what we should do if the necessity arose—placed a spar, possibly the mast of the boat, from end to end of the shieling as a ridge pole, and used the sail or a tarpaulin for a roof. The outside shape of the building is such that the roof could be held down very neatly with stones and turves. I found remains of old fires and semi-charred bones of sheep and sea birds when digging out the floor.

There is one art common to the houses of Rona, the beehive shielings and the black houses of the Outer Isles,

PLATE 7

FIANUIS, RONA
The hut can be distinguished at the left-hand side

an art carried intact from the mists of antiquity. It is in
the set of the flat stones of which all these buildings are
made. Each stone is highest at its inward edge, so that the
slope is downward and outward. If this technique is carried through from floor to roof, it is possible to bank up
the outside with turf without any fear of wet trickling to
the inside. The crystalline surface of the stone and the
very nature of the unplastered dry-stone walling prevent
actual dampness being apparent. A good black house is
draught-proof, of a healthy dryness inside, and condensa-
tion is unknown. This art in building the walls of a dwelling allows of the placing of a thatch roof in such a way
that it appears to outrage common sense; the thatch
extends only a little way over the inside edge of the walls,
and as these are always three feet thick or more, there is a
terrace between the foot of the thatch and the outer edge
of the wall. The terrace forms a favourite dog shelf in the
Outer Isles and the goodman of the house and his friends
will themselves occupy it as a comfortable resting-place
on summer evenings.

There is a type of structure on Rona which I do not
understand. One of them is on the low, bare peninsula of
Sceapull at the south-west of the island and the other is on
the east side of the cultivated area below the chapel. It
consists of four pillars of dry-stone, set at the corners of a
six-foot square. The height is not more than four or five
feet now and the pillars themselves are about two or three
feet square. The inhabitants of some of the Shetland Isles
used to build open stone sheds for drying fish and it is
possible these stone puzzles of Rona were 'skios' also.
Rona is almost a museum of curious works in stone, for
there are the piles dotted along what appear to be random
lengths of one-course stone dyking. Mr. Malcolm Stewart
suggests that these were foundations for stacks of dry turf
and I can accept this explanation for those on the ridge and
above the village, especially when the places can still be
seen where the turf was cut. But those carefully built little

rings of one course of stone, spaced so regularly along the
dyke, seem to me more puzzling. The turf is thick all
about and I can detect no scars such as those just visible
north and west of the village. We have found several
quern stones buried about the village and two fragments
of stone vessels. These we have placed in the west end of
the chapel, which might as well be Rona's museum for the
present.

The cell of St. Ronan and the chapel built on the west
end of it are the heart of Rona. They probably form one
of the oldest Christian buildings in Britain remaining in
their original state, and it seems strange that the fact of
remoteness should have been the cause of inertia on the
part of either the state or the ecclesiastical authorities.
Here is something unique in Christian history and it is
falling to ruin, partly through neglect and apathy, and
partly, I believe, through occasional visitors to Rona
ferreting among the stones for that rare bird to be mentioned later, Leach's fork-tailed petrel.

The cell itself is probably twelve hundred years old and
represents the finest example I know of that technique of
dry-stone walling shown in the black house and the beehive shieling. If St. Ronan built it himself, as seems
likely, he was a man of his hands as well as a man of prayer
and mental strength—for he must have been strong intel-
lectually to have lived alone on Rona. The floor of the
cell measures 11 feet 6 inches by 8 feet, but immediately
the side walls begin their thrust inwards until at a height
of over 11 feet they are less than 2 feet apart. The final
roof-covering is of oblong slabs placed transversely and
most of these are still in place. The stones of which the
inside walls of the cell are composed are flat slabs of
Hebridean gneiss of varying thickness and size and quite
undressed. The fitting of the stones is a thing of beauty to
one who thinks he can build a dry-stone dyke. Such spaces
as there are have been wedged with small chips of stone so

that the final surface is practically flush. The roof has fallen or been removed from each end of the cell, but I have replaced the few stones necessary at the west end and have banked up the earth there so that it should remain sound for a few more years.

The inside surface of the cell has been plastered with lime and sand at some period and part of this facing remains. It seems to have been put on with the fingers, for it shows many little semicircular depressions which fit my fingers, placed as they would be in doing such a job. When carefully examining the eastern inside wall of the cell I found a deuk of pine wood still plugged into the wall. The wood is sodden and almost rotten, but its original shape is intact because the plastering of lime fits round it exactly. A piece of wood in this position would probably not last five hundred years, and if this surmise is correct the plastering must have been done within the comparatively recent history of the cell.

The floor was covered with earth and stones and a fulmar petrel nests in each corner of the cell during the breeding-season. It would be unwise at the moment to excavate this floor completely because the northern wall has cracked vertically in two places, causing the central portion to sag inwards. Some thoughtful body in the past has wedged two long stones on end between the floor and the wall and I imagine they now carry a fair strain. My own work in the cell has been confined to its eastern end. The urgent need of this remarkable building is to have two or three hoops of iron fitted inside, following the cross-sectional shape of the cell, with transverse strappings of iron bolted to these. The work of clearing the floor and strengthening the outside could then proceed without fear of the walls falling in and the work of St. Ronan's hands being lost for all time.

There is a small, longitudinal window in the upper part of the west end of the cell, going through to what is the east wall of the chapel. There is also a doorway at the foot

of this wall. Muir spoke of this as 'a square doorway . . .
so low that you have to creep on your elbows and knees',
and his sketches give the impression that this was the
original height. The sketch of the inside wall of the west
end of the cell given in Mr. Stewart's book also gives this
impression because the floor appears as being paved. I
looked at cell and chapel a long time and tried to imagine
St. Ronan crawling indoors. My own long experience of
crawling through an opening of similar height into a bell
tent in wet weather made me decide that even a saintly man
and an ascetic would not have endured such an exasperat-
ing method of getting in and out. It was this opinion
which decided me to dig in the chapel.

The chapel is rather larger than the cell and gives the
impression of being much larger because the inside walls
are perpendicular. The east and west walls, being gable
ends, still remain the highest, the west one being quite
eight feet. The north wall has fallen as low as two to three
feet in the middle, and it is evident from the set of the
courses remaining that the whole wall has listed outwards
and warped. Entrance to the chapel is by a low doorway in
the south wall, but when I first went to Rona all the outside of the very thick wall near the doorway had fallen
outwards. The inside had also fallen badly, but the innermost lintel stone was still precariously poised and gave the
true height of the door.

I brought with me to Rona a copy of Harvie-Brown's
Vertebrate Fauna of the Outer Hebrides in which there is
a photograph taken on the occasion of his first visit in
1885. This was probably the first photograph taken of
the chapel and certainly the only one published at this
early time. Its interest to me, therefore, was very great,
for it showed the south wall of the chapel to be standing
a good six feet high. A remarkable bulge or increased
thickness was evident in the eastern half of the wall beyond
the door. Having this photograph to work by, I felt justified in clearing the fallen stones outside the southern wall

of the chapel and rebuilding to the level shown in the photograph taken over fifty years ago.

I began nervously, for I hardly knew how much I had undertaken and I feared any necessity of pulling down before I could rebuild. Confidence soon came and there was something encouraging in knowing I should be using the same stones that had been the original wall. The foundation was at last clear in the neighbourhood of the door-way and it was evident that the eastern side of the wall was several inches thicker than the western and projected farther outwards. I built on the foundation shown and reached the lintel height at my waist. The lintel was raised little by little by lifting each end and my son putting stones underneath, until I could at last slide it into position.

The stones seemed to come to my hand and I had hardly ever to handle one twice. It was a task of excitement and pleasure which satisfied me when it was finished. Except for one or two stones which have been buried and are not covered with lichen, I cannot see where the old work finished and mine began.

Chickweed, grass, and silverweed were growing on the floor of the chapel which was high and uneven with the accumulation of fallen stone and earth. I did not begin excavations until the fulmar petrels had left, because I felt they had a certain right to the place by regular occupation for many years. My first aim was to determine the true level of the floor at the door-way between cell and chapel. Its height was even further reduced since Muir's day of 'elbows and knees'; only the fulmar petrels could creep through to their young in the corners of the cell.

When I had gone down a couple of feet and was clearing my way at the sides of the door, my spade struck a mass of stone from which came a few grains of lime mortar, showing pink on the brown earth I was moving. I continued with greater care and soon laid bare a square mass of well-built masonry in the north-east corner of the chapel. This had at one time been plastered all over with lime mortar. A similar pillar was revealed at the other side of the cell door-way, but this one did not extend as far as the corner of the chapel.

I now dug out about a third of the floor of the chapel, taking my cue for depth from what I should find at the cell door. It was evident that a clay floor had been beaten into position in the chapel at a level a few inches below the top of these pillars of masonry which I took to be the supports for the wooden plank which we learn from the minister of Barvas (quoted by Martin Martin) formed the altar in the chapel:

'There is an altar in it [the chapel] on which there lies a big plank of wood about ten feet in length; every foot has a hole in it, and in every hole a stone, to which the natives ascribe several virtues: one of them is singular, as they say, for promoting speedy delivery to a woman in travail.'

There was a deep layer of sand beneath the clay floor, and when it is remembered that Rona has no shore and that the nearest white sand is in small patches on the storm-beach of Fianuis, the labour of getting it to the chapel must have been great. I cleared the whole of the chapel floor to the level of the clay, which must have been the floor the ancient race took care 'to keep it neat and clean, and sweep it every day'. The clay itself must have been imported from Lewis, where there is some in the parish of Barvas, for the soil of Rona has no clayey texture.

Still digging downwards in the door-way I struck hard ground 4 feet 4 inches below the lintel. It was at this level also that the altar supports began and I found a rough stone paving extending from the inside of the cell door-way out across the chapel. There was no point in following up this initial stone paving, because the sand and clay floor of the chapel above it was in itself of archaeological interest and value. So I have built a course of stone right across the chapel to prevent the clay floor falling into the portion excavated at the east end. The door-way of the cell

PLATE 8

a. EAST END OF THE CHAPEL, RONA, AFTER EXCAVATION
The doorway leads into the cell

b. QUERN STONES, NOW IN THE WEST END OF THE CHAPEL, RONA

and the flanking altar supports are now clear to the old paving. I have not dug far into the cell at the western end because of possible subsidence, but there are signs in the section laid bare that there has been more than one floor in this place. Large numbers of bird bones and a few of seals have come to light from the paving level under the sand and some show charring. I have found no artefacts of any kind unless one radius bone of a gannet has been used as a skewer or pointed tool. This bone is about nine inches long, pointed at one end, and the shank is very highly polished. Although it must have been buried there for hundreds of years and is stained a permanent brown, the surface reassumed its brilliant smoothness as soon as it was dry and I had rubbed off the dirt.

Muir's sketch of the cell indicated an altar-stone at the east end of the cell, but this had disappeared when we first went to Rona. It seemed to me that if Muir had not gone below the 'elbows and knees' level, his altar-*stone* might be the top of the altar only, and I felt justified in excavating the east end of the cell. This was exciting work, for I laid bare an altar of good masonry 3 feet long, 2 feet 6 inches high, and 2 feet 3 inches deep. The top stone was lying at right angles to the altar under a layer of earth, but I have put it back into position. The paving in front of the altar is in sound state and on the same level as that of the door-way. It is evident that a slightly raised step a foot wide ran round the edge of the floor along the walls.

As I was digging at floor level beside the south side of the altar my spade was deflected from a rounded stone which, even in the dim light of the cell, showed green. My first thought was—Iona marble—a stone with which I am familiar, for I always carry some small pieces in my pocket. I picked up the stone, washed it, and found a piece of smooth, dark-green marble about the size and shape of a sheep's heart. There was an intricate veining of lighter green. No rock of this kind occurs naturally on Rona, and, found in this place of all others, I wondered if

St. Ronan had been to the college of Iona and had brought
this piece of stone to his church on Rona to be a symbol of
the mother foundation. Dr. Douglas Simpson of the
University of Aberdeen, who is an authority on early
Christian remains in Scotland, tells me that pieces of
stone of foreign origin have been found before in cells of
the first Christian period.

This stone has left Rona with me, so that it may be seen
by antiquaries and men of science, and that it may not be
lost. But it must go back to its place as part of Ronan's
altar and not be kept by me or placed in a museum. I have
left a token of good faith of my present custodianship by
burying three of my own pebbles of Iona marble in the
masonry of the altar. Fanciful, perhaps, but it has pleased
me so to do.

It seems certain, then, that St. Ronan entered his cell
like a decent Christian with no more than a stoop and a
sideways twist through an opening 4 feet 4 inches by
1 foot 8 inches. When I sit by this ruined chapel among
the lazy beds it is not difficult to imagine the life of a
happy people. Imagination of St. Ronan was more difficult within the dark, dank cell before I dug. But one thing
brought him alongside us—the little aumbry, a few inches
square and neatly built near the eastern end of the south
wall. The impression, now that the altar has been cleared
and the full height revealed, is of a simple, early church of
great dignity.

Muir described and pictured a rough-hewn cross of
gneiss bearing three holes, one each in head and arms,
which was standing in the burial-ground. This cross
was still there in 1885, because it can be seen distinctly
standing west of the chapel, in the photograph in Harvie-
Brown's book. It has now disappeared from the burial-
ground and I was much grieved when I could not find it
on Rona. Writing of my disappointment to Mr. Malcolm
Stewart drew from him the interesting information that he
had found the cross in the churchyard of Teampull

Mholuidh, Eoropaidh, near Ness in Lewis. He has also kindly sent me a photograph of the cross which shows it to be in a better state of preservation than the ones remaining on Rona. There can be little doubt that the men of Ness lifted the cross from Rona, and we may hope that if the Royal Commission on Ancient and Historical Monuments and Constructions of Scotland implements its recommendation of 1928, the cross will be returned to its right place.

There are three crosses remaining in the burial-ground; one has almost lost its head and arms by weathering and the other two are in little better state. The best of them is a double cross about 2 feet 3 inches in length and 1 foot broad across the arms. None of them bear any signs of inscriptions or ornamentation and in their anonymous quality, their smallness, and ruggedness they are fitting to the seclusion of Rona. Other stones which have doubtless been crosses remain at the heads of the graves.

I have said the cell and chapel are the heart of Rona. Every island has a heart, and when men live on it they find the heart and build their dwellings near it. There is usually some good reason of shelter or accessibility to the shore and fresh water, but sometimes the reason is not as plain as that. Once that heart has been fixed by the men of old time, it remains as such to later comers like ourselves. It was interesting, for example, to find the foundations of an ancient dwelling appear under the wooden hut we put up for ourselves on Eilean a' Chleirich. The place had been boggy and it was not until I drained it that the shape of the earlier building came to light. That place is the only one which feels home on the island and no other site would do at all. Our hut on Rona is in the little sheep fank at the neck of Fianuis. The spray blows across that neck in times of storm, so that grass is scarce and the herbage is mostly chickweed and poa grass. It is a good place for us, close to the seals on whose behaviour we are working, and with a magnificent outlook. We are well satisfied, but it is strange to find that, independently and unconsciously at first, my wife, the child, and myself would visit the area of the chapel and village some time during each day. The day did not seem complete unless we had been to the heart of the island, sat about under the wall and watched and listened to the surf rolling over the low rocks of Loba Sgeir and breaking on the skerry of Gealldruig Mhor. The social quality of men is not confined to meetings here and now; it extends through time, passing on its leaven through simple works done in lonely places.

The coasts of Rona are rockbound and man can do little to alter their appearance, but there are two small things he has done which will last a little longer yet. A ring and staple have been let into the rock in Geodha Stoth and are now rusting away. It was weeks before I found them. The other is a short iron bar let into the rock near the water-level at the extreme south-west corner of the island, by the narrow sound of water called Caolas Loba Sgeir. Hot lime has been used in securing this bar and two small stones are lying in the mortar. Despite the rush of water through the channel in a north-westerly gale, this ancient type of cement is as sound as ever and the bar will never come out until it rusts off. No one would moor a boat in such a position except for an hour or two on a very calm day, and then only a dinghy; the reason must be farther to seek, and my own suggestion is that a fish or seal net was slung across in earlier times when Rona was inhabited. Martin Martin describes such nets as being in use in Harris and Uist in the seventeenth century.

This essay may be of service to future visitors to Rona, and for that reason I will describe the ways of the sea in relation to the possibly difficult task of getting ashore. There is almost always a swell about Rona and it is often of a confused type which makes it hard to let down a boat from a small ship, however easy the actual landing on the rocks may be. The best landing is Geodha Stoth on the

PLATE 9

a. THE CHAPEL AND CELL, RONA, JULY 1938
From the south

b. THE SAME, SEPTEMBER 1938

east side of the island, and the water here can be extraordinarily calm when there is a gale blowing from the
west or south-west. Similarly, if a heavy south-easterly
gale is running, there is good shelter for a ship in the west
bay. The floor of the east bay is rock, and a ship's anchor
will not take good hold; constant watchfulness is therefore
necessary. Landing of gear is easiest from Geodha Stoth
because there is a sheer ledge against which a launch can
come with safety, but if the wind is south a swell creeps
round Sron na Caorach below the Tor and can soon make
landing impossible in the geo.[1] An attempt may then be
made in the next small inlet farther north, Langa Beirie,
where a point of rock breaks the sea from the south and
south-east. The farther into Langa Beirie a launch may go
the calmer it is, but the harder it will be to get stuff ashore,
for the cliff is sheer. Great care should be taken in watching for occasional big swells which will lift a boat on to the
rocks. It is no good trying any farther north, as the rock
shelves dangerously and the sea will be no quieter.

A landing is possible on the south side of the Sgeildige
Geo, west of the tunnel cave, when the western ocean is
free from swell and there is wind from the east or south-
east. Once on to the ledge there is a climb of fifty feet or
more up the cliffs which are too steep for anything else but
personal gear. Marcasgeo on the south-west is also calm
in an east wind, but the ship from which the boat was
lowered would have to lie rather far out and it is not the
sort of place a master would like. The south shore is the
most regularly bad for landing, and the only reasonable
place is on the *east* side of Poll Heallair. I emphasize the
east side because Harvie-Brown and others have given the
west and from my experience that is bad or impossible.

---

[1] *Geo* means a small narrow inlet in a rocky shore. The word occurs
in Gaelic and in the Scandinavian languages, and as it refers to a definite
kind of place for which there is no single English word, it is time geo
came into the language. It is an everyday usage in Shetland, Orkney, and
the West Highlands and Islands.

There is a fifty-foot climb up the cliff on the east side of the geo and it would be difficult to get heavy gear up there. Nevertheless, it could be done with men enough and there is the advantage that it is the nearest landing to the chapel and ruined village.

The sea about Rona is nowhere as regularly calm as in Geodha Stoth. This geo will have very little swell sometimes, even when there is an immense swell breaking on the west. It is a surprising fact, because the south side is very bad with swell even when the wind is in the north. When there is a north wind Geodha Stoth is impossible. The size of the waves is gigantic at such times and the observer on Rona will see but two swells between Leac Mor and the cliff below the Tor. A week should be allowed for the sea to settle before landing is attempted after a bad northerly gale. The swell will be bad for days in Geodha Stoth during the winter-time, whatever the airt of the wind, and Rona is then absolutely isolated. We have seen a month go by without one day fit for landing.

We have built up the dyke on the west side of the sheep fank on the neck of the Fianuis peninsula and though this place looks to be in danger from the sea it is not. A northwest gale coming direct into Sgeildige Geo sends clouds of spray over the neck of land, but the tunnel cave and the northern side of the geo act as a safety valve and take a great deal of water. There is also a deep cave going in under the neck and reaching as far as the fank, and this cave also takes a lot of water. The dead sheer cliff at the head of the geo seems to turn the water into the caves where the force is broken. There is also the constant backwash from the geo and the caves which prevents the sea coming green over the neck.

A northerly gale does not unduly upset a camp in the fank, for the rest of the peninsula and the storm-beach break the seas, and to a slight extent the wind. Fianuis becomes an inferno when a big northerly or westerly gale is blowing. It is certainly not safe for a human being to go looking at the wonderful spectacle of wild sea. The water climbs up the steep gullies on the west side of the peninsula and at a height of fifty or sixty feet above the sea has still sufficient force to roll boulders up and down which may weigh anything from a hundredweight to two tons. Both the boulders and the bedded rock are scarred anew each winter. Immense seas break over the cliffs as far as the storm-beach and spray rises twice or thrice the height of the cliffs. The spray breaks the full three hundred feet of height of the western cliffs of Rona in a winter gale and is driven right over the island.

North Rona is a green island. It must have lain remote in its waste of ocean for an even longer period than the Hebrides have been islands, for here there has been no such growth as to make possible the deposition of peat as on Lewis and the mainland. Soil overlies the rock to a depth of a few inches and that provides for the vegetation of Rona. The rock itself is impervious, and because the unbroken hill gives no hollows for the water to stand for long, the slopes of grass drain the water to the cliff edges. Wells of two or three inches' depth are dotted about the island, and in times of heavy rain there is a run of water west of the village, draining to the west of Leac na Sgrob. This water is always brown and from April to September tastes of the birds which regularly bathe in it. The best well of the island is an artificial hollow in the solid rock near the edge of the cliff at the head of Poll Heallair. The position of the well marked on the Ordnance Survey map is too far inland. Stones have been built over the well and we have left it covered with a large stone. The water is clean and good and the drip is constant, but in winter it is a little brackish because so much spray is driven over the island.

Although no water stands for long on the main mass of the island, its slow and constant drainage towards the sea through such a shallow soil keeps the turf well watered so that it remains green in the driest spells of weather. A botanist may be disappointed with the flora of Rona, for it is singularly even and the species are comparatively few. The main herbage floor is composed of bents, Yorkshire fog, and sheep's fescue, with plenty of white clover where the ground was cultivated. A few sedges appear north and west of the village where the turf has been removed in earlier times. Yellow flowers of the hawkbit appear here and there but are nowhere common. Scurvy grass grows luxuriantly on the bird-haunted cliffs which are frequently rimmed with sheep sorrel and mayweed.

The peninsula of Fianuis is much more interesting botanically. The majority of the great black-backed gulls nest here and the ground is heavily manured by them. Constant washing by the salt spray imposes a decided limit to the range of plants which can thrive there. Annual poa grass appears at the foot of the hill ridge and extends thinly where there is any vegetation on the peninsula. Sea milkwort is also common, but the most striking growth is the chickweed of which there are several acres. It alone seems able to take advantage of the high manuring, and the thickest areas on the east side of Fianuis reach to the height of a foot. This chickweed is relished by the few sheep which graze on Rona, and the five grey lag-geese which have been here all summer appear to feed on it to the exclusion of grass. There is still far too much of the plant to be eaten down and a mat of it rots every year, so that in some places there is now a peat layer over a foot deep. The surface of Fianuis is more broken than any other part of the island, and this fact, together with the chickweed peat, allows of many stagnant, brackish pools which are the breeding-ground of hordes of Chironomid flies. The drier parts of Fianuis are made gay with great mats of sea pinks. The passage of thousands of seals over the face of the peninsula makes a swamp of the area covered with chickweed, and the northern face of the hill is in little better condition.

Fianuis is perhaps the most interesting part of North

Rona to the biologist, despite the impressive quality of the bird cliffs. I have never been sorry that we made our camp in the sheep fank on that narrow neck, for the peninsula seems to be the gateway of the island where we see most of what is going on. Fianuis catches the migratory birds and many of them can feed there better than anywhere else on Rona. It is here that the waders come, to feed on the fly larvae in the brackish dubs and about the expanse of rough, sea-worn rock which is Leac Mhor. Knots were common during the first half of September, though these birds are rarely seen in the Outer Hebrides. Redshanks are resident, but there was an influx of what I took to be Iceland birds in September. I saw a spotted redshank two days in succession at the end of September. Dunlins are there in summer and on migration; sanderlings appear on migration, and ringed plovers also. It was on Fianuis I saw a green sandpiper, some little stints, and a woodcock, and—of all things—a turtle-dove.

Several flocks of about thirty white wagtails appeared at the end of August and were about us for a month, but they were to be found nowhere else but on Fianuis. A few swallows and swifts came for a week in July and they acted in a way I have seen before on little islands where we have been the only inhabitants. They have flown round us at very close range and followed us in our walks, as if they, having adopted human habitations, were glad to see human animals in this houseless place on their journey.

The turnstones of Rona call for special mention. They are to be seen on the seaward rocks of Sceapull and Loba Sgeir, but the mass of them, perhaps two hundred in all, live on Fianuis. Few stones are small enough for them to turn, though the belt of flat wrack on the sea-washed rocks is regularly and vigorously chucked over by them at each low tide. We reached Rona on July 12th, which was too late to hope to find eggs, but I believe the turnstone breeds on Rona. They were numerous when we first went there and many were in the brilliant breeding plumage.

I saw families of three young birds following pairs of
adults on several occasions and sometimes they made
begging movements, as if they were the children of the
pairs. I can hardly think they had migrated south from
the tundra regions by that time.

Turnstones did not appear when I was working on the
seals of the Treshnish Isles, but on Rona I think of them
as the little companions of the seals. The very habits of
the turnstones altered when the grey seals came ashore in
September. These busy little people almost forsook the
intertidal zone and worked round the seals instead. The
great beasts would go into the dubs of water and churn
them up thoroughly, then they would flop out and dry.
The tide they had made in the pool doubtless left many
tiny creatures stranded on the edges and the turnstones
were not slow to take advantage of the harvest. They also
inspected the seals themselves and assiduously turned over
any seal excrement they could find. The seals accepted
the turnstones and I never saw one snap at the little birds
as they do sometimes at the gulls if they come too close.
This companionship with the seals was a habit of the
turnstones only and did not extend to the redshanks and
dunlins which were fairly common. Sometimes the purple
sandpiper would come into the seal grounds or a group of
knots in early autumn, but I never saw them so close to the
animals or so busy as the turnstones. The purple sandpipers, however, do join the turnstones in the winter-
time in working over the morass which the seals have
made. I have hopes of returning to Rona in the spring and
establishing the fact of turnstones being resident.

I think it would be safe to say that nowhere else in
Britain is there such a large colony of great black-backed
gulls as on North Rona, where there are between five
hundred and seven hundred and fifty breeding pairs.
These are strikingly handsome birds in their sharp black
and white plumage and yellow beak, and it is something
of a spectacle to sit on the north side of the hill on Rona

PLATE 10

PUFFINS, RONA

and see them dotted about Fianuis in such large numbers. They almost exclude the herring gull and lesser black-backed gulls, of which species there are only very small flocks, and the eye becomes so accustomed to these giant gulls that the lesser species look quite finely made in comparison. The raucous din made by the black-backs is the one bird noise of which I get tired. Everywhere you go it is a complaint, a protest, a growl at your being there.

The black-backs of Rona form a migratory population, coming there to breed and feed while the hosts of puffins are ashore and then away again. Some return when the seals breed because there are dead calves to be eaten and plenty of afterbirths. Puffins form the staple diet of the black-backs in summer here and the toll must be a heavy one. Suppose there are a thousand black-backs on Rona and each takes a puffin each four days—a very conservative estimate—that would mean two hundred and fifty puffins a day for the whole ten weeks of the breeding season, a total of fifteen to twenty thousand birds. And yet there appear to be just as many at the end of the time as there were at the beginning. Each pair of puffins rears only one chick a year, so to maintain the population and serve as a food supply for other birds as well, it seems likely that the puffin's possible life is a long one.

Puffins excite our sympathy because of their mingled solemnity and ridiculousness. Their calm, dark eyes indicate a serene philosophy—though we are not entitled to make that interpretation—and it is easy to fancy about them a patient resignation to the destiny of being a food supply. The puffin and the rabbit, indeed, have much in common. The black-backs hunt the puffins at the burrows in the early morning and at the evening time, not by any dashing swoop, but by a dart of the great beak as the puffin emerges from its burrow. It is distressing to see two black-backs trying to gain possession of one puffin, for the poor little bird is often pulled in two. The cliffs of Rona are littered with the skins of puffins neatly pulled inside out from the carcass as a glove would be drawn from the hand. Such is the technique of the black-back.

The peregrine falcons take and eat their puffins in a different way: a quick flight along the cliffs, uttering a harsh bark, and clouds of frightened puffins issue forth to make their seemingly pointless little circular flights over the sea. The falcon takes her choice and stoops and the puffin is dead. She flies with her quarry to a dub of water, wets the feathers well, and then plucks them from the skin. Soon a cleanly picked breast-bone with the wings attached is all that remains of the puffin.

The storm beach on Fianuis provides an environmental factor allowing the black guillemot and the Arctic tern to breed there, the former deep among the ramp of boulders and the terns in the open on the sandy, pebble-strewn places. Pebbles of hornblende gneiss are very like terns' eggs, and the nests and young are difficult to find. Until the terns went away in August there were only the two hours from midnight when the terns were quiet. The high, chittering scream, coming incessantly from a black-capped head poised between indefatigable wings! That is an island sound lying deep in many a mind.

Both the north-eastern and north-western cliffs of Rona seethe with birds in summer, but I think the west provides the most wonderful spectacle. It is sheer, and there is a magnificent red column in the middle of it rising unbroken to the top at three hundred feet. There are thousands of guillemots here, thousands of puffins and thousands of kittiwakes; hundreds of fulmar petrels and hundreds of razorbills; an immense vocal concourse until August, when suddenly the guillemots will disappear in a night, then the puffins will go and the kittiwakes will follow more gradually. The cliff becomes silent.

All these birds strike the eye and ear in the daytime, but they are not more wonderful than Rona's birds of the night which are the Leach's fork-tailed and storm petrels. The stormies are old friends of our island years, but the fork-

PLATE II

a. THE SKERRY OF GEALLDRUIG MHOR: SRON AN T-TINNTIR
IN THE FOREGROUND

b. VALE, RONA, 22ND DECEMBER 1938

tails were new and exciting. They nest at three places only in Britain—St. Kilda, the Flannan Isles, and North Rona.

We used to make midnight journeys to the chapel and ruined village on fine nights in July, my wife, the child, and I, and enjoy a natural concert which few people ever know. The half light of the summer night, the boom of the swell on Loba Sgeir, and the quietness of the village. Then a flying shape flits through the air, close to us and without sound. Quietness again. Then a strange, staccato laughing cry comes out of the air, and from somewhere among the stones and turf dykes there rises a sweet, ascending trill, beautiful to hear. The swift-flying shapes increase in number about the ruins and the volume of sound grows. Excitement is in the air and you can feel it waxing in this community of little black birds. Their flight is erratic and swift in this aerial dance, and when two or three hundred are flying in this way within a restricted space, collisions are common. Our faces were brushed by the soft wings smelling strongly of the characteristic petrel musk. A pitch of excitement is reached after one o'clock in the morning and the laughter and erratic movement wane before the dawn. Each night of summer sees and hears this natural wonder, but Rona lies 'afar off in the lap of wild ocean' and the world is a busy and serious place where the life of little petrels is of small importance. I have attempted the almost impossible in trying to photograph the birds by flashlight in the midst of their ecstatic whirl; there are the images on the film, but not good enough for me to give you here. Another year, another try, perhaps; it would be a thing to treasure.

We come back silent to the hut on the neck of Fianuis, a little sleepy and awestruck. But we are not alone; the storm petrels are churring comfortingly among the stones of the fank and the fork-tails which live in the storm beach and beehive shieling are still crying their strange laugh into the North Atlantic night.

This is Rona.

IV

THE SOCIAL LIFE OF ANIMALS

WHAT are the causes of animals gathering in flocks?

This is a much more difficult question to answer than—what advantages accrue from animals gathering together?

The questions can be answered in broad outline in the following way before going on to describe types of social life more particularly. Animals are caused to gather in numbers for the purpose of reproduction; the food supply may be of such a type that they are caused to flock in seeking it; in the lower animals where large numbers of eggs are laid together it is natural that the young when hatched should be found together, and many organisms cannot exist solitarily or in small numbers, for there is a partly unknown factor acting physiologically.

Advantages of social life are obvious, but they should be largely looked upon as effects and subsequent developments of animals' being together, and not as *reasons* why they gather. It is improbable, for example, that a number of sheep scattered about a hill-side and frightened by a passing aeroplane would flock together because they had any idea that as a flock they would be better able to withstand this unknown thing which is consequently a possible danger. It is much more likely that the presence of possible danger makes solitariness an unpleasant sensation and the animals feel better individually for being with others of their own kind, though there may be nothing helpful they can do when they are together. Human beings often act in this way long before they assure themselves that they have gathered for the social advantage of strength in union. From this primary blind urge the musk ox of Northern Greenland has built up the extremely well-ordered social habit of forming a close circle, cows and calves to the centre and the horned heads of the bulls facing outwards from the circumference.

The advantages which develop among the higher animals from living together include the strength which comes from union, which makes the whole greater than the sum of its parts; co-operation and division of labour; the easier development of intelligence and the possible growth of a tradition which in itself has a high social value; the growth of a code of behaviour which may have ethical qualities; and the freedom given for the trial of variations which might be dangerous for the continuance of individuals.

I do not intend to touch on the specialized social development of insects, nor am I going to deal with aggregations of the lower animals generally; but it will be as well to mention the physiological advantages of numbers which are evident, because they show the deeply rooted nature of sociality in animal life.

Professor W. C. Allee of Chicago has done much work on this subject and has gathered together a variety of data in his book *Animal Aggregations*, 1931. Tadpoles, for example, which have had their tails lopped off, regenerate them sooner if they are in company than when solitary. Small fish can better withstand poisonous conditions in their water if there is a goodly number of fish present. In these instances it is found that the waste products of metabolism have a value in making the water a better medium for growth or reducing the toxicity. Medium densities in culture bottles of the fruit fly *Drosophila* thrive better than either high or low densities, and in this instance it is more difficult to point to the controlling factor.

Here are two observations of my own which show the dependence of some species on maintenance of numbers. The sheep blowfly or greenbottle, *Lucilia sericata*, lays its eggs in the wool of the sheep, and when these hatch the larvae feed first on the sweat or 'swint' at the base of the wool fibres. Their waste products set up an irritation of the sheep's skin and they are very soon feeding wholly on the living flesh. I have spent many gruelling hours searching sheep for these terrible pests and removing the close masses of maggots. In such circumstances there is neither time nor the inclination to be experimental, but in my island years I have had different conditions in which to work. There is no enclosed place on Eilean a' Chleirich in which an affected sheep could be kept, and if I have found a maggoty ewe or lamb I have had to put it on a long tether until the great patch of raw skin has dried over. This has enabled me to watch very closely the mode of attack of the fly on such a sheep.

The female flies do not strike the sheep singly. There is a gathering of six, ten, or a dozen at one place, and the eggs of all of them are laid very close together or even in one mass. These many hundreds or thousands of eggs hatch more or less at the same time and their subsequent growth is very rapid. Now if almost all these maggots are removed at an early stage and only a small number left, say six or twelve, they do not survive but die in a few hours. They die in the midst of plenty and it is quite evident that a high density of blowfly maggots is favourable to their growth in every way.

Scottish hill sheep in out-of-the-way places which are not regularly visited by the shepherds are beginning to learn how to rid themselves of blowfly maggots. They will go to a peat hag and rub the affected part free of wool, and to a large extent free of maggots. But it is inevitable, as I have found, that some maggots are left unharmed; yet these do not survive unless a considerable pocket of them is left in close association.

This dependence on numbers is undoubtedly of a chemico-physiological nature. The maggots thrive by stewing in their own juice and the whole condition made by the aggregation is necessary for the individual; his own contribution is not self-sufficient.

The following example is on a higher plane. The female buff-tip moth, *Phalera bucephala*, lays her eggs in a neat mass, one deep, on an oak leaf. When they hatch the tiny caterpillars do not disperse but mass together in a more or less circular patch on the leaf. The egg cases having been eaten and the dermal layer of the leaf, the mass moves on to a fresh patch of leaf; and so they must keep on moving when they have exhausted the food immediately beneath them. They grow a little bigger and now we find that when a new patch is reached a very thin web of silk is woven over the mass of caterpillars at each place where they stay to feed. If a single caterpillar or a very small number is put on a leaf it will be noticed that the feet have a very poor hold, and the caterpillar is knocked off with the slightest wave of the branch. That web of silk binding the mass together is very slight, the contribution of each individual must be extremely small, but the whole structure is sufficient to bind them to the leaf, and it is much more efficient and economical in time and material than that which each caterpillar could spin for itself.

There is still another social advantage of the gathering of buff-tip caterpillars, not a mechanical one this time, but a visual effect which must save them from the keen eyes of small birds. As the caterpillars reach a length which is approximately half the width of an oak leaf the groups become smaller, varying from ten to thirty in each. They lie side by side and tail to tail along the veins of the leaf, heads to the outer edge where they feed, and tails to the spine of the leaf. This arrangement makes for an excellent protective patterning, and when that leaf is exhausted the caterpillars move as a party to the next leaf and rearrange themselves.

My own observations have taken me no farther than this, and as I seem more and more to spend my summers in treeless surroundings I cannot see when I shall be able to learn more of the buff-tip caterpillars, but many readers of this book who have the time, patience, and ingenuity will be living in an environment where buff-tip moths are common, and perhaps they will find out some of the things which for the present must remain unknown for me. At exactly what ages do the large groups break up into smaller ones? What exactly is the behaviour of the group about to move? And when rearrangement takes place along the spine of a new leaf, do the caterpillars have definite places, or is the position of their immediate companions purely a matter of chance?

I cite these examples of sociality from among the lower animals to show the far-reaching tendency of animals to forgather, and the influence it has on simple lives quite unlike those of the birds and mammals.

It is such data as these, worked out in much greater detail, which have led Professor Allee to the view that co-operation towards a common end can be used as a criterion of social behaviour, and he has taken as a basis for his own definition of sociality the primary acquisition by animals of a tolerance for the presence of others of their kind within a limited space. He sees the many advances in evolution which may have come about through the selection of such co-operating groups, rather than through the selection of individuals. In the book already mentioned he has written: 'This implies that the two great natural principles of struggle for existence and of co-operation are not wholly in opposition, but that each may have reacted upon the other in determining the trend of animal evolution.'

This is a clear and beautiful concept: let us keep it in mind as we see something of the lives of higher animals which are social.

Animals have a sense of property, and this is primarily directed to the occupation of the ground over which they feed and on which they breed. Such observations lead to the notion of territory as an important factor in the lives of animals, and it is one of the foundation stones of sociality. Territory and range are quite different ideas. The one is

PLATE 12

CLIFF FACE, RONA. GUILLEMOTS ON THE LEDGE AND
KITTIWAKES ABOVE AND BELOW

very real and personal to the animals themselves; the other is quite unknown to them, and range is a fact which mostly interests human beings who wish to know the geographical distribution of species. Territory exists within range and for the student of social behaviour it is more important than range, because it has to do with the intimate daily lives of the animals.

External factors of environment such as climate and food supply govern range, but territorial boundaries are often decided psychologically by animals, and they have, it might be said, a nice eye for topographical detail. By observing the limits of a territory animals are able to get the best out of it. They know the easiest ways about the ground, where they are most likely to get the largest supply of food, and where they can lie in greatest comfort and safety. Sometimes they have to fight to maintain their territorial boundaries, but only rarely, for animals are usually content. Nomadism, also, is not normal in nature; indeed, it may be called pathological.

The fact of territorial observance in itself makes for animals gathering in groups in which they know each other, but it is not sufficient to make for the semi-permanent and complicated social systems which we find to exist in mammals and in a few species of birds. The great binding force is reproduction and its associated processes. Let us consider the life of the Scottish red deer in some detail to illustrate this statement.

Here is a species which has solved a big problem very neatly in the course of evolution. In a grazing animal the herd becomes a bulwark against danger, and within reason it is advantageous that a fairly large number of the animals should be together. Mixed gatherings of the two sexes in an animal society are apt to lead to quarrelling between the males, and the final state is one of small groups each headed by a male. Such a patriarchal group has distinct limitations in relation to the species as a whole, because in the first place the group cannot be very large.

Sexual jealousy is always present in a patriarchal society, and though a male animal may attempt to keep a large number of females, he is not successful because the females either wander away from him or the ground covered by the group is too extensive to allow of the male being at both sides of the territory within a very short space of time.

Secondly, the sexual jealousy of a patriarch causes him to drive forth the young males at an early age, so that they are deprived of a period of maternal attention and education which they might otherwise enjoy. The devotion of an animal patriarch to his group is not commonly wholehearted and selfless.

A very different state exists in a matriarchal society. Here the female is the leader and her leadership is very largely influenced by her mother love. Her group is not one which repels fresh numbers, but embraces them. The limits to numbers in a matriarchal society are not of a psychological nature so much as environmental, for the matriarch is not encumbered with personal desires and jealousies—at least, not in a herd of red deer.

This matriarchal state has been reached in this species by a segregation of the sexes for all the year except the six weeks of the breeding season. The stags beyond the age of three years gather in loose companies on territories, the boundaries of which are fairly well observed. I say loose companies because no single stag appears to take on the responsibilities of leadership, nor is there any leadership, and there may be considerable variation in the numbers running together at any one time. A stag will occasionally winter with one company and summer with another. Such lack of cohesion within the company does not influence the cardinal fact that there are stag grounds and hind grounds with long histories as such, and the grounds continue to be occupied by stags or hinds in the face of a fair amount of pressure which man may bring to bear on the deer.

The hinds form very closely knit groups on sharply demarcated territories. Here and there the winter territories of hinds and stags may overlap or cut across each other, but that is not the general rule. Summer territories are very often communal and are situated on the high ground. This does not mean that the sexes or different groups are closely mixed at this time; they keep very much to themselves but graze over practically the same area.

The hind groups tend to grow in size and sometimes bud off small new groups if the population as a whole is increasing. This is quite different from the conduct of a stag company, which may be compared with a school where the numbers remain approximately the same, but the personnel changes from year to year. The hind group is a social entity founded on the family, and there is always a leader who is a mature hind with a calf at foot. Her supremacy is not challenged and the herd follows her actions with close attention. I do not remember ever seeing a leading hind which did not have a calf of her own, and I think the active motherhood in which she is involved plays an important part in her leadership; the maternal protective quality is extended to the whole group. A hind which was barren or ceased to be a regular breeder would never reach leadership, or would naturally relinquish it. The young deer of both sexes remain with their mothers for three years; then the staggies leave the hind herd but the young hinds remain in the group. Education, therefore, is protracted and tradition is strong.

Hinds suckle their calves the year round. Such persistent lactation is indicative of an active anterior pituitary gland and, as Dr. Wiesner and Miss Sheard have shown experimentally for the rat, in their book *Maternal Behaviour in the Rat*, a supply of the hormone of this ductless gland can initiate and maintain maternal behaviour. The social life of red deer is profoundly influenced, then, by reproduction, and whichever way the subject of sociality is studied, it is evident that reproduction plays a major part, though not necessarily in the way of the deer hind and her group.

I could recount many beautiful examples of the constant nervous watchfulness of the leading hind for her immediate family and the larger group, but I will give only one which is quite clear cut, and could not be flavoured by any previously conceived ideas I might have had in my head.

There was a small group of deer in a hollow opposite my house, and for some winters I took them a little food every afternoon. They never became tame, unfortunately, and they used to stand some distance off and watch me put down the corn and move away. The lie of the land was such that they could see me return to my house, and they usually liked to see me well on the way before they came to the food.

One evening I put down the maize and lay ten yards away hidden in the heather. The five deer were longer than usual in coming down, and when they did the leading hind was not free from nervousness. She stopped five yards above the food, muzzle raised, while the others trotted down to the corn and began eating greedily. She was as hungry as they were, doubtless, but she remained walking to and fro for two minutes, then moved a few yards uphill where she could see the top of my head. This caused her to move her head this way and that to gain slightly different views of me, and what she learnt was enough to send her a few feet higher where she could see the whole of me.

Then she barked, once.

The four deer threw up their heads immediately; I being so close to them and to the ground, heard their feet come together before they ran up the hill to stand near the leader. They stood stock still by her for some seconds, during which time I felt more and more foolish. There they were, twenty-five yards away, looking at me sprawling in the heather. I got up and walked away, and

PLATE 13

KITTIWAKES AND YOUNG

because they knew me well enough they did not run in the other direction. It was a few minutes before I reached our little white house on the opposite side of the glen and where the deer could see me.

I put my glass on them and watched. The pattern of my return was now completed and I saw the leader trot down *first* to the scant remains of the food. The others followed her.

Anybody who intends to watch deer successfully must make sure which is the leading hind before attempting to stalk close to a group. Any animal may give the alarm, but none so likely as the leader; if her head is up the stalker must remain frozen. That watchful mother of the herd has fully earned the title given her in the forest country—'herself of the long neck'.

The voice of the hind is a short, sharp bark, which carries a long way and has the immediate effect of putting all the deer on the alert. But when the need for alarm is present, not all the hinds bark; only the leader, or the one which first became aware of the disturbing factor. What a refreshing discipline in the exercise of the female voice!

The least socially minded members of the hind group are the young stags below three years of age. It is surprising what liberties can be taken with them in approaching deer. All the same, when these young beasts leave the maternal group they become much more wary. It has often been observed that in the summer season an old stag will be accompanied on the hill by a youngster newly shed from his mother's territory. This youngster appears to take on the duties of watcher while his elder takes his ease. If I and many other observers are not wholly mistaken there is a social bond here between males which is not commonly found in the larger companies of stags. Such an association would be for the summer season only, for with the coming of the rut the big stag would be away to the hind grounds, and would not tolerate the near presence of his little friend. Stags in winter and spring frequently group together in age classes, another social manifestation which goes to show that the community life of higher animals is complex and not just a matter of aggregation.

There is a third and strictly seasonal grouping of red deer to be found at the rutting time. From mid-September to the end of October there is an apparent modification of the matriarchal state when the stags come singly to the hind grounds and attempt to segregate a number of hinds for themselves alone. The stags demarcate small rutting territories on which they herd their hinds very much in the way a collie dog rounds up sheep. The boundaries between each stag's territory may be a burn, a dip in the ground, or some other small change in the nature of the ground. The behaviour of the stags towards each other is described in another essay, for here we are mainly concerned with their conduct within their temporary territories.

There is no doubt that the stag attracts more attention to himself from an observer of a harem than do the hinds. He is so often on the move, trotting round his hinds and making a lot of noise, and superficially he seems to be earning the title of 'Monarch of the Glen' which Landseer gave to his picture of a great rutting stag. I believe that title and picture have coloured the imagination of many people and caused them to believe that a stag is truly master at this time. Closer observation and a little experimental interference will show that this is not so.

The interest of the stag in his harem is purely that of sexual gratification. His actions are those of keeping out all other stags—even the two-year-olds still running with their mothers are temporarily driven to the outskirts—and of keeping in the few hinds he considers to be his. It will be seen after a period of critical watching that the hinds are impassive to all this show of force; they are constantly tending to stray beyond the boundaries the stag has set.

I have said there is an apparent modification of the

social system at this time, and the fact that it is more apparent than real is shown when the herd is disturbed—say, by the observer. The stag himself has not taken part in any of the routine watchfulness which is characteristic of the hinds, for his interest and activity are self-centred. When disturbance takes place the leading hind barks and the group of deer gathers round her preparatory to moving away. She leads them; if she stops to look back to see what is happening, the herd stops also, and no member goes in front of her; she is unquestionably the leader. It is very possible that the hinds in adjacent harems are also of her group, and they join up with her regardless of the stags.

And what is happening to the stags? Jealousies forgotten in what appears to be the common danger they take to their heels and go their own ways, which may be with the herd as insignificant individuals without responsibility of leadership, or they may run away on their own, feeling no loyalty to the harem they were herding so spectacularly but a minute or two ago. The dominance of the stag, then, is not that of the monarch. The matriarchy is maintained.

As far as I have been able to judge from my own observations, roe deer follow a patriarchal social system of a much less highly advanced kind than that which I have described above.

The roe deer is a shy woodland creature, not commonly found in numbers but in twos and threes and occasionally as many as six together. They have their own territories, doubtless, but I have never been able to delimit them as I have those of the red deer. Roe deer are constantly shifting their ground and it is not possible to forecast accurately where they will be from day to day. When the buck is with the group, which is very often, the observer may see that the does and fawns tend to follow him and that it is he who takes on the duties of extreme watchfulness. The yearling fawns are not encouraged to stay with the parents, and if they are males they are chased out by the buck. These little yearlings are slender threads of their race to be wandering about alone or in twos and threes. Here, then, is none of that family cohesion and strength of the herd as a unit which is so impressive in the life-history of the red deer.

I should not wish to strain the comparison and base an opinion on these two species only, but I believe that a social system of the matriarchal type in animal life is a distinct evolutionary advance on the patriarchal. Patriarchy sets a definite limit to gregariousness in grazing animals, and because this system is never selfless it is apt to hinder a close social life. Matriarchy, with its fundamental principle of mother love and constant tendency to embrace rather than repel, can move forward towards a development of an ethical system. It is far from unknown for a hind to take another calf to suckle as well as her own if its own mother should die. As we have seen it in the red deer, matriarchy requires the separation of the sexes for a large part of the year and the male is relieved of parental care.

The life story of the Atlantic grey seal, as I have observed it on remote islands off the West Highland coasts, is the subject of another essay in this book, but I shall give an outline here of the social pattern of this species to show the great contrast with the sociality of the red deer, and to indicate the complexity of social behaviour as a whole in the higher animals. The Atlantic seals are loosely gregarious throughout the year and for much of that time the bulls and cows mix together indiscriminately. All the same, I have noticed a tendency for adult bulls to mass together on certain rocks where the animals lie out of the water.

The focal point of the grey seals' social life is the breeding ground. The number of places where these seals breed is strictly limited, and off Scottish coasts the breeding grounds are a few remote islands many miles distant

PLATE 14

A HAREM OF ATLANTIC GREY SEALS
In the pools of the erosion platform at the south end of Lunga, Treshnish Isles

from each other. Although the seals may be widely distributed in spring and summer, the breeding stock must return to the small, traditional islands, and there is perforce a considerable aggregation of the animals at these places.

The mature bulls leave the water before the cows and take up positions within areas they consider their territories. Each bull has either a tiny bay to himself, a length of shore perhaps twenty or fifty yards long, or if he comes far up from the sea he may have a more or less circular territory not more than a few yards across. The bulls lie quiet in their chosen places, none challenges them at first and there is no advertisement of the breeding territory such as we saw in the harems of the red deer.

Cows gradually come ashore and join the bulls, though sometimes a bull may wait weeks before any cows come to his place. My experience is that the bulls do not wait in vain. A bull without cows, lying in his territory adjacent to another where cows are present, makes no attempt to encroach on his neighbour's ground or steal his females. He just waits. If challenge should come it will not be from a neighbour but from a bull fresh from the sea who has as yet no territory. The social behaviour of the breeding season is based on territory more than upon personalities, for the bull seems primarily concerned in preserving his particular bit of ground, rather than keeping any cows within it. For example, I have seen an amorous cow turn away from a lazy bull and go into a neighbouring bull's territory where she received immediate advances. All well and good, there was no quarrelling about that, but when a strange bull emerged from the sea within the lazy bull's sphere of influence, he was chased away by the lazy one, who was now stimulated to remarkable activity and agility.

There is no reason why the grey seals should come far ashore unless they are going to breed, for away from the sea or wave-washed rocks they are in danger. A prominent feature of a seal nursery, especially on North Rona, is the neutral territory of the breeding stock. There may be four or five hundred seals gathered in one place there on the flat rocks of the sea's edge. The animals lie cheek by jowl and there is comparatively little quarrelling. Large numbers of bulls in full breeding condition are content to be alongside each other without any show of animosity. Yet, once those same bulls go inland to take territories from early males now growing tired, they would fight very seriously.

The large area of neutral ground with its little pools is a very important place in the social economy of the animals, serving as a reservoir of bulls and of cows not quite at the calving state, and as a 'buffer region' not subject to the conventions or the possible dangers of the breeding territories two or three hundred yards inland. Some of the immature seals may join the breeders on the neutral ground, but they do not take part in the migration inland. Indeed, on Lunga of the Treshnish Isles, where most of the calves of that race of grey seals are born, the young seals of previous years are not to be seen at all. Their migratory rhythm is different. The number of immature seals to be seen on Rona is not as great as the expected total population of the one- to three-year-olds, and it is probable that many of them do not return to the breeding ground till they are mature, but remain feeding about the Hebridean and north Scottish coasts.

Sociality may be a potent factor in the evolution of new races and eventually of new species. We have seen that the red deer hinds keep rigidly to their own territories and inbreeding of a very close nature is prevented by the travelling habits of the stags at the rutting season. Nevertheless, the social system is close enough to result in well-marked characteristics of size and antler growth being apparent in different forest areas. Such differences may be environmental to a certain extent, but they are also genetic.

The tendency of sociality to isolate races is even more

evident in the life of the grey seals. First, there are the few traditional and widely separated breeding islands. I believe the seals of one race and another may actually overlap in the course of their summer migrations about the tortuous Highland coasts, but there is no evidence yet to show that there is any true mixture of races because the breeding migration in autumn takes them back to their ancestral grounds. Second, the close territorial habits of the bulls and the tendency of the cows to come up to the same place to calve each year make for the development of clans. The natives of North Uist say the grey seals of the Sound of Harris are different from those of Haskeir, two stations not far apart. And now, after a close study of the two widely separated races of grey seals on the Treshnish Isles and on North Rona, I can say that there are well-marked differences between them.

I will describe now a totally different kind of social group—a colony of herring gulls consisting of a large number of pairs of birds observing monogamy throughout the breeding season, and possibly throughout life. Winter flocks of gulls may be composed of young and old birds, but only the adults repair to the traditional gulleries, usually in March. The advent of the gulls is not sudden; they appear in gradually increasing numbers during the month, which tends to show that the adults have probably not kept in the same flock through the winter months. The full complement of the birds may not be present until the third week of April. Roosting at the gulleries begins about March 15th.

The course of the social life of the herring gull can be more easily described if I take as a concrete example the largest gullery on Eilean a' Chleirich which I have watched for many hours of many days. This is a triangular area of about one and a half acres of deeply broken cliff-top; the sea is on two sides and the top of the cliff between forty and fifty feet above the water. The steep angle at which the stratified Torridonian sandstone lay allowed of numerous small pools of water forming within the gullery.

Once more, territory is of very great importance to this concourse of birds. The flock is a unitary whole, but within it each pair has its own private nesting territory which is kept inviolate by the male bird. There is also an area along the cliff edge devoid of nests and considered by the birds as neutral territory. They gather here in close and amicable communion for part of each day, the periods thus spent becoming shorter as the breeding season advances. It seemed to me, as I watched my birds in the early spring, that they came to the island paired, and when roosting there began, they were certainly in pairs at bedtime.

The herring gulls are fairly closely massed on their gullery, much more so than the lesser black-backed gulls farther inland, but less close together than is common in black-headed gulleries, where the nests are so near that there is a considerable amount of anti-social behaviour.

A German worker, Dr. Goethe, has described the relatively close nesting-habits of immense flocks of five thousand pairs of herring gulls which he has studied, and he saw many examples of anti-social behaviour which were certainly absent among my birds. I suppose a direct comparison might be made here with human affairs. Small communities are almost free from serious crime, but in large, unwieldy masses, real sociality is lost and numbers mean mere agglomerations in which crime is frequent. I do not remember one instance of egg-stealing or chick-bullying among my small flocks.

In addition to this decent behaviour of my herring gulls among themselves I have witnessed examples of a fairly common phenomenon—sociality between species. When the lesser black-backed gulls arrived on the island at the end of March they rested for several nights on the neutral cliff-edge of the herring gullery, and were not molested. The same thing happened with the few pairs of common

PLATE 15

COMMUNITY OF GUILLEMOTS, RONA

gulls which nested on Eilean a' Chleirich; though a smaller species they were allowed to rest in the herring gullery until they left to take up their own nesting sites.

The broken area of the cliff-top provides a variety of knolls and hollows, and each pair likes to have a tiny knoll and the few square yards round it as a nesting territory. The knoll itself becomes the standing-place of the male bird and he delimits the territory round it. There is no truer adage than 'every cock has his own muck-heap'; male birds do like a bit of raised ground on which to stand at the breeding season and advertise their presence. The members of the pair display to each other within their territory and, as I have described in another essay, there are certain communal displays which may take place over the gullery or on the neutral ground.

Each pair has its own private life, but the life of the flock is there also. The wealth of sound and movement among birds of their own kind or of similar species is a stimulant to the emotions of each bird, and there arises a synchronization of action which may be carried forward to the physiological field of egg-laying. I have written of this aspect of the social group in the essay on display, but in this place I wish to show the benefit to the group of the synchronization of breeding which results from the social habit. At least the numbers of the flocks on Eilean a' Chleirich and the survival rates among the chicks have led me to this conclusion.

During my first year of watching these birds there were four colonies, numbering ninety, thirty-four, twenty, and four birds respectively. I found that the large flock began laying slightly earlier than the smaller flocks—May 7th, May 12th, May 18th, and the four birds did not reach the stage of laying though they built nests. It was much more surprising to find that the larger flocks laid their total crop of eggs in a shorter period than the smaller ones—seventeen, twenty-three, and twenty-six days respectively. Similar, but not quite such striking results, came from my second year of watching, and the same phenomenon was also found to be at work in the lesser black-backed gulleries. The possibility of these figures arising from chance is statistically remote. In each flock hatching dates corresponded with the dates of egg-laying, i.e. twenty-three days afterwards.

What, then, is the survival value of egg-laying and chick-rearing throughout a flock occupying a shorter time? Herring gull chicks are preyed upon by other birds, particularly by great black-backed gulls and, on Eilean a' Chleirich, herons. The chicks are taken when in the down-feathered stage, not after the quill feathers have sprouted, so that while chicks in down are present they are liable to attack. There are about five pairs of great black-backed gulls on this island, and they take as many chicks as they please without much opposition from the flock as a group. If, therefore, the members of the chick crop of a colony are all in the down stage at more or less the same time, the danger period for the colony as a whole is shortened. The toll taken by a constant number of predatory birds will be a smaller proportion than in colonies where there are chicks passing through the down stage for a much longer time.

The facts led to this conclusion, for when the fledgeling age was reached in these colonies, the largest one yielded nearly half of the chicks hatched; the second colony fledged just over a third of its chicks, and the third colony only a little more than a fifth of the chicks hatched. There was a colony of three pairs in the second year, which hatched eight chicks, but only one reached fledgeling age. It is apparent, therefore, that the social habit in these birds has a distinct survival value for the species.

We have looked into the social life of animals which live in permanent herds or gather in seasonal aggregations for the purpose of breeding. But there is also the sociality of migrating animals and of winter flocks of birds. Migration appears to be one of the great causes of flocking, though such companies do not attain to the complicated social systems of breeding communities.

Sociality in greater or lesser degree is part of every animal's life and any study of animal behaviour which ignores it must be incomplete. Solitariness is almost non-existent. Even the eagle, a hunting bird which must have its own private beat, is far from solitary or satisfied with the companionship of its mate. I have seen the four pairs of eagles from fifty thousand acres of the forest country gather together over a remote glen and indulge in a magnificent display of aerial playfulness; and this more than once.

A solitary animal is a rare thing to find and is always ill in some way or other. Careful experiments designed to rear chickens solitarily have shown that such birds soon become neurotic and, to all intents and purposes, insane. It is in the very nature of animals to crave company, and this accounts for some of those pathetic, affectionate relationships between lions and lambs and elephants and mice which arise in the unnatural environments of menageries. It is not just because we are human that we like dogs and horses about us. Our humanness may make us lonely in the presence of our fellows, but it is the animal in us which craves companionship of the simple kind which may be devoid of intellectual contact.

The social pattern of a species may have to be fulfilled before the cardinal process of reproduction can take place; and yet, how far does the subject receive mention in zoological curricula or in the science which emanates from laboratories? Until we are prepared to go to the animals and find out their relations with each other our biology must be moribund and deny its very name.

V

RON MOR: THE GREAT SEAL

MAMMALS do not provide the opportunities for us to study their life-histories in such close detail as do most of the birds. They are much more shy in their comings and goings, and many have nocturnal or subterranean habits. The number living wholly above ground and not actively hiding is very small, and these animals have the compensation of fleetness of foot, intensely acute senses, and a developed shyness. Our knowledge of British mammals is distinctly anecdotal in quality, and a student of animal behaviour will find few researches giving a continuous story of animals' intimate daily lives comparable with the good work which has been done on birds. The task imposes development of more cunning techniques, a fusion of the cleverness of the laboratory with the elemental craft and awareness of the primitive hunter. There is here a rich field of research which will satisfy aesthetic, academic, and practical ends.

Our task becomes even harder when an animal lives for all or part of its life in a medium where it cannot be followed and inhabits places which are always difficult of access. How little we know of the behaviour of Leviathan! We see him for the momentary and regular period of his roll and blow as he pursues his ocean path, or we see him in flight and pain from the deck of a whaler. Sometimes, as I have written elsewhere in this book, the great beast may be seen at ease, idly nosing about the remote foot of island cliffs. These are glimpses, moments of wonder when a veil is lifted, and sometimes there is an interpreter like a Melville who can save them for the world. Read the full passages again in *Moby Dick* from which I quote these few sentences:

'Stealing unawares upon the whale in the fancied security of the

middle of solitary seas, you find him unbent from the vast corpu-
lence of his dignity, and kitten-like, he plays on the ocean as if it
were a hearth.'

'But far beneath this wondrous world upon the surface, another
and still stranger world met our eyes as we gazed over the side.
For, suspended in those watery vaults, floated the forms of the
nursing mothers of the whales . . .'

But we cannot follow them through the vast country of
the oceans, and the order of their civilization remains a
mystery for our questing minds. The enormous face and
tiny eye of Leviathan tell us nothing of the workings of
that much-convoluted, high type of brain which lies behind
the mask.

We are in somewhat better case with the seal tribe, for
they are original animals of the land which through the
aeons of evolutionary time have returned to the ocean for
their sustenance, and have almost become adapted for a
permanent life therein. The adaptation is not complete,
for seals must come ashore to breed.

The Atlantic Grey Seal, the *Ron Mor* or great seal of
Gaeldom, is more shy than the little seal of the firths and
the eastern coasts of Britain, and of all our mammals it is
the one about which we know least. Its home is the wilder
Atlantic shores and its breeding-place the more remote,
uninhabited islets where human beings will pay no more
than fleeting visits. To these places I have followed *Ron
Mor* and watched part of the animals' lives. I have
watched them on the dry land and from the tops of cliffs
where the eye can see deep into the water. I have learned
something of their happy lives in the sea. But the wholeness of their life story remains unknown to me and I can
see years of work ahead. What are the paths of their
migrations to and from the isolated breeding-grounds?
How wide does the stock of each island range? Do the
seals of each breeding-ground form closed cities, and if
so, are there the occasional wandering adventurers moving
between the cities as are found in the nations of men?

When do the great seals first breed, and to what age do they live? All these things are hidden as yet and I am challenged anew each time I see the strength and calm dignity of the mature bull seal's head breaking the surface of the ocean. Where is our dignity and serenity to compare with his? We are but Peeping Toms into the lives of his people and he preserves the fine indifference which we lost when we became human. We find ourselves compelled to go on seeking, but let our reflective power govern our findings and redound to the good of the creatures on which we spy. Man the seeker need not be for ever man the destroyer.

The animals have outlawed us and show us fear whether there be need or no. At best there is that indifference in the face of a friendly advance. When the deer come down and pass by in long strings before the coming of deep snow they are indifferent to our presence but ready to fear, and the great seals ashore on Rona attain an indifference, but they are not regardless. When a sheep passes through a group of seal mothers, strange beast though it may be to them, there is an acceptance of its presence which is denied to most of us. And how rarely will a wild animal let us help it in time of trouble!

My heart is with them always, and when I come up against that barrier of indifference and readiness to fear, I suffer for the generations of men who have harried and slaughtered. If I could speak and the animals turn their heads in pleasure; if I could offer my hand and they touch it with their delicate muzzles, I would then be happier and less lonely. It seems our lot to watch the lives of animals only by stealth and artifice, and our right has gone to approach them in amity as lowlier brethren of the same earth.

But as I live longer in the lonely places of the islands there come moments of compensation. The great seals of Rona accept me as those of the Treshnish Isles never did. It has been grand and inspiring to go down to the sea's

PLATE 16

A FAT, SLEEK BULL, NEWLY ARRIVED FROM THE SEA

edge and see two or three hundred seals come racing through the water in joyful movement towards me. I have found the way to speak to them so that they are not afraid, but pleased. Those old bulls of the great dignity remain on the outer ring of the group of faces, though one of the biggest of them will come close in. The cows are nearer to me, their expressions soft and inquisitive, but the yearling seals have the wondering faces of little children, and in their confidence they have come out of the water to my feet as I have sat there on the rock, using my voice in the way I have learned. That secret of the voice which will bring them is mine alone and will remain so, lest it should ever come to be misused. At these times I do not carry camera or binoculars for the seals do not like them; nor do other animals for that matter. One day I called a blind cow seal out of the sea and she came near until her muzzle was but a few inches from my face. She was unafraid and returned quietly to the sea. And now the mother seals are high on Rona near the door of our hut and our own child plays among them. They seem neither to resent nor fear, but to accept him as part of the indigenous fauna. The little calves themselves are more afraid than their mothers, and they will not play.

The seals are diligently fishing during the summer and they do not spend very long periods out of the water. There are not many of them in the neighbourhood of the breeding-grounds, for they spread over much of the West Highland coast-line. But those which do remain about the nursery islands, and the first lots of immigrants in August, do not come out of the water at the places where they will come ashore to breed. The seals gather on skerries offshore which have now attained a traditional significance. More and more come there in August and September and they spend increasing periods out of the water. Then individual bulls will leave these places and take up positions alone at places on the island where the cows will come later to have their calves.

There is at first a majority of bulls on these waiting-rocks; then many cows come, and some of the bulls are going ashore. The cows follow in due course after a week or a fortnight, and still more bulls gather at the waiting-rocks, which become reservoirs of bulls when the breeding-season is at its height. I have described this aspect of the seals' life in another essay in this book, but in an impersonal fashion; come with me to Leac Mhor of North Rona, which is the main gateway of the seals on to this island, and the greatest reservoir throughout the breeding-season.

Leac means a slab or flattish expanse of rock shelving into the sea, and Leac Mhor, the great slab, on the east side of Fianuis is the only place of its kind on Rona. It is Leac Mhor which has made the island the metropolis it is for the Atlantic seals, and therefore given Rona its name —Ron-ay—seal island. How ancient must be the civilization of the seals in this place! The island was called Rona long before St. Ronan adopted the name for himself when he went to live there in the eighth century. Here, without doubt, is a capital city of well-marked ways older than the cultures of Sumer and the valley of the Indus.

Two gullies run inland from Leac Mhor and reach almost across Fianuis. This is the centre from which most of the cows spread to have their calves, although a large number comes up from Geodha Stoth as well. It is easy for the seals to get ashore on Leac Mhor, and even when there is an immense swell running well over this expanse, the surface is sufficiently broken to allow the seals to hold on and not be sucked away again in the backwash. There are many definite tracks where the seals come on to Leac Mhor and work up the gullies. They appear to be worn just as old stone steps are worn by the constant passage of feet, but I am not prepared to believe outright that the bellies of countless generations of seals have worn these places. Probably they are natural drainage channels made by water through a period which would make the city of the seals look young.

The seals lie together in great masses on Leac Mhor. I have tried to count them sometimes, but have got lost at something over four hundred, because I know there have been many out of sight. There is another skerry north of Leac Mhor called Sgor na Lice Moire where another three or four hundred may be counted, and north again about the stark rocks of Lisgeir Mhor and Boghannan there are three hundred more. There is a continuous crying in that falsetto *crescendo-diminuendo* which has, I think, been over-romanticized. The sound is a grand one at the breeding season in the stillness of the night, but if you are crawling through these rocks with me and watch the seals while they are crying you will see their raised hands with the claws hooked, ready to make a quick scratch on their neighbour's hide. And yet these bickerings are not serious, just the rough and half-playful remarks of people jostled in a crowd, because until there are territories to be guarded and calves to be cared for, there is only present position and comfort to argue.

The great seals massed on the rocks make a wonderful pattern for the eye. Some are dry and showing light-coloured, some are dark, and those which have newly come from the water have a glossy sleekness throwing back the sunlight, and they appear darker than they really are. It is one of my surmises that each nursery ground of the Atlantic grey seals becomes a closed city, and that the seals of the Treshnish, for example, will have been racially distinct from those of Rona or of Hasgeir for a very long period. Slight differences between the races will tend to be perpetuated through time, and this particularly with such a variable character as coat colour.

The bull seals on the Treshnish Isles were all brown in colour, a curious olive brown that was like the tangle itself. Indeed, when a Treshnish bull was lying among this weed at low tide he was almost indistinguishable from it. The throat and belly of the bull seal are but sparsely flecked with white; his crown is a lighter colour than his back, sometimes appearing a bright ginger. The bulls of Rona are mostly steel grey in colour and only a few are brown like those of the Treshnish Isles. They have very little white on them and their crown is of bright metallic grey. Some bull seals are almost black, and though no white or lighter-coloured crown appears on these, it is possible to distinguish a dapple pattern in the coat when dry, which is very similar to that showing through the coat of some brown horses. It is extremely beautiful and lustrous, but the black bulls are very few and I saw none at all on the Treshnish Isles.

The cow seals are light grey in colour on the back, and in it can be distinguished a skin-dappling or flecking of black. The throat and belly are white, boldly splashed with black, which now extends to the hair itself as well as the skin beneath. No two seals are alike in their patterns; some have very little black and in others the white may become isolated spots in a black ground. I have seen wholly mole-coloured cows on Rona and on the Treshnish, and in each place has appeared one bright ginger cow with black-flecked throat. Such rare beasts are very striking and of remarkable beauty. There is one cow seal on Rona which has a skin of an even dove-grey colour and her muzzle and the backs of her hands are black. Only once have I seen a bull of as light a grey as the cows; he lies out on the rocks at the north end of Rona.

The coats of the young seals are as variable as those of the adults, though about the time they are yearlings the coat seems to have faded to a pale dappled fawn and they all look very much alike until they moult again. When they are out of the water and dry the light is refracted and they appear almost white from a distance. A young seal can be told very readily by the fact that it has no throat and belly splashings of black.

Imagine, then, the varied pattern of hundreds of seals on one small skerry, a blue ceaseless sea at its foot and the sun shining on dappled coats of a dozen colours and

PLATE 17

ATLANTIC GREY SEALS ON LISGEAR, RONA

patterns in themselves. It is exciting and amusing to creep close among them. You can see the thrutching movements as they change position, the ridiculously human gestures as they scratch with their fingers at head, palms, or belly, and smooth their whiskers this way and that, quickly, with the back of the hand. I call their fore-paws hands because flippers indicate rather the mittened limb of the whale. The seal's fingers are distinct and the hand is prehensile and very like our own in use. Watch also the way of the hand when it is that of a mother scratching or playing with her baby.

I have lain there for hours among the seals. They are resting, in a way, but they are never wholly still. And there is always sound—the long cries, and the little noises, the sneezes, and the rumbles within their great bellies. Some come up from the sea, others go down to it; some will splash or bask in the tiny pools left by the tide, and the little turnstones search diligently among the great beasts. The air itself is acrid with the scent of the seals, an old, old smell of the sea and of animal warmth. Some-times a bull will half recognize my presence and will look at me in doubt and reproach as it seems, but he forgets and loses interest in my immobility and, passing his hand over his face like an old man, sinks back into sleep. If a cow sees me she will act in fundamentally the same way as a red deer hind; she will come nearer me to make sure, and having done so will go down to the sea.

I would not wish it to be thought that I never frighten the seals, but when I do it is usually because I come on some of them suddenly or on the occasions when I am going my ways about the island and they get my scent from afar without knowing where I am. Whether it be deer or seals or any other animal that uses its nose, scent without knowledge of the position of its source is very frightening. I have seen Leac Mhor become a seething mass of undulating movement, of hundreds of seals hastening for the security of the sea. It is a wonderful sight, but it gives me no pleasure.

The seals which come ashore to breed in Geodha Stoth do not make Leac Mhor their waiting-rock. They lie out on the ledges under the Tor and in Geodha Mairi. But an east or a north wind makes this impossible for them and they go over to the big skerry of Gealldruig Mhor, where they may stay until the wind gets round to its favourite airt of south-west. Then they come back again into the east bay of Rona, and I was once lucky in seeing the great joyful crowd return. They came back playfully, undulating through the surface-layer of the water in obvious enjoyment. A happy, romping people on the move, where the children could tease the old men with impunity; an ancient people in their ancient home, but not yet grown tired with civilization. The great seals are the people of the sea, and it is not to be wondered at that Gaeldom should have invested them with a half-veiled but occasionally irruptive humanity.

Many are the queer legends and stories of the sea people, always oblique in allusion, always leaving something unsaid; analysis and direct explanation might be profanity. What does the old ballad say of the grey silkie (grey seal) of Sule Skerrie? It tells a story in that sad, fatalistic way of the ballads in which the bond between the seals and men is felt. A woman is nursing her foster child and wondering about its father, when she finds a 'grumly man' beside her who speaks thus:

> I am a man upo' the lan'
> An' I am a silkie in the sea;
> And when I'm far and far frae lan',
> My dwelling is in Sule Skerrie.

He says he will take his son one day and teach him to 'swim the faem', and ends with the prophecy that the woman will marry a 'proud gunner' who will 'shoot baith my young son and me'.

PLATE 18

FEEDING TIME: ATLANTIC GREY SEAL COW AND DAY-OLD CALF

Incidentally, there are now no seals at Sule Skerry, the flat rock which lies midway between North Rona and the Orkneys, nearly fifty miles from each. A lighthouse was built there in 1893, and though the common seals do not bother much either about a lighthouse or a foghorn, the grey seal will not stay in their presence. Perhaps the grey silkies of Sule Skerrie moved to Orkney, where the species has become more numerous in recent years.

There is another story of a man who struck a bull seal on the head from a boat and caused the animal a great wound. He landed on an island at a later time and met a hermit with a long scar through his hair, and the man knew what he had done in his wanton act. The stories of changelings are common in the Isles, and for those who know the baby seals well the tales are easy to understand. There is no creature born, even among the great apes, which more resembles a human baby in its ways and its cries than a baby grey seal.

Come with me to the seal nursery on the erosion platform of igneous rock at the south end of Lunga of the Treshnish Isles. If we lie on the cliff sixty feet above them we can see the family life of fifty seals and their babies. The newly born ones are there clad in cream or ashen coats of long fur. How long seem their arms and legs at this time! It is surprising with what ease they can move about, and some of them move too far, perhaps to the sea's edge or to another mother, and either course means danger. But their loose skins begin to tighten as the little people fatten within a day or two, and the calf lies on its back for long periods with little more movement than to wave its hands and feet now and again and cry for its mother when hungry. I have even seen a baby seal holding its fingers in its mouth. Some of them find the safe pools on the platform where they swim happily from the time they are two or three days old. Play with their mothers in these pools is particularly beautiful to watch; both enter into it fully.

An idyllic quality pervades this gnarled platform when the tide is low of a late September afternoon. Because the tide is low there is plenty of room, and activity among the mothers is slight enough to bring a halt to their expressions of jealousy. Danger seems far away, and yet danger is never far from the sea's edge. I have written elsewhere in this book of the great seals' mastery of their element, that they will seek and enjoy the immense Atlantic surf of Rona. In form their adaptation to the ways of the sea is perfect, but the cardinal process of reproduction chains them to the land and the frontier of the sea's edge. Their gathering in large numbers for the breeding season at a few small islands, and their inability to move rapidly and easily on land, lays them open to dangers they never meet in the ocean itself. But there is the peril of the sea at this time as well as of predatory man and other animals. It is on these out-thrusts of rock at tide level, on the southern ends of Lunga and of Bac Beag or 'the little Dutchman', where the Atlantic storms come unhindered from the south-west, that danger for the seals is to be seen most dramatically.

How often in my work with the seals have I found a storm to come at about the time of the spring tides! The seas almost cover the rock platforms at these times and the great waves break and run as far as the foot of the cliff. The seals and their young are compelled to mass together on a small area still above tide level, and their constant jealousy is not overcome by the common danger of the waves. Each cow is thinking only of her own calf and she lies below it to break the impact of the surf and to prevent the calf being sucked away in the cruel backwash. The patience and diligence of the mothers is very great at these times; the method also is good. Some of the babies are inevitably caught by the inexorable, unpredictable waves and are tumbled about unmercifully in the tumult of ocean and rock. They are washed high and tiny hands grip desperately to the smooth rock which will give no hold. Back they are rolled, over and over, and bruised against the boulders; then up again for another attempt to get out of the clutches of the sea, away from those cruel, licking tongues of water. But this is that same element in which they were lately playing happily. It, in its turn, is tortured by the impelling tyranny of wind. Sometimes I have found these drowned calves after a storm and it is pitiful to see the grand failure they have made. Finger nails are worn away to their roots and palms and chins are rubbed raw from the constant effort to climb out.

I have pulled the babies from the surf myself once or twice, but I have also tried and failed. There was the day-old calf of a very young cow in the Sgeildige Geo of Rona. How it got there I do not know, but its mother was inexperienced and her behaviour showed the limitations of blind maternal affection. There was a heavy surf and the sheer cliffs there hold no more sanctuary for a seal than a few ledges often washed by the waves. That mother got below her calf and lifted it so that it could climb on to a ledge, but the surf was great and many efforts were needed. It got out, but within a few moments was washed back again. Then I saw the mother lift it between her hands and hold the calf against the ledge so that it could climb. Time after time the waves sucked it away and the baby's cries were piteous.

This young mother was losing interest. She began to play with the calf, rolling it to and fro and taking it below water in her hands. To put it uncritically and anthropomorphically, the calf seemed now to have much more sense than its mother—it was fighting for its own little life without a knowledge of its whereabouts. Dusk fell; I went down the cliff on a rope which my wife held from above and I got on to a ledge where the calf had tried once before and where I hoped it would come again. The night was now too dark for me to see far, but I could hear the cries of the baby among the noise of water. It came nearer and I saw the black eyes in a little white face. I grabbed with both hands as the sea came up round me, but that wave was so sudden in its rise and fall my fingers got no hold in the wet and slippery fur of the baby seal. It passed out of my reach and hearing, and for us the pounding of the surf in the caves beneath our hut was a terrible sound that night, one from which we yearned to get away. Had I got the calf I would have put it in a saucer-like hollow on the shelving rock on the north side of the geo and hoped for the best.

This danger of the sea to the species when the young are born is lessened in time by a very wonderful modification in animal growth. The mothers come ashore two days before calving and are then in a very fat condition. Henceforward they do not feed until the calf is three or four weeks old. The growth of the calf, therefore, is dependent wholly upon the body of its mother, and this growth is extremely rapid. After that first day or two of activity when the calf unfolds itself and establishes its muscles, it moves very little, but lies on its back and sleeps. The calves are tubby at a week and of an almost incredible fatness at a fortnight old. Their coat of white fur is fluffy and a little shorter than it was at first because it has worn down in these two weeks. And now it begins to be shed, at first from the face and limbs and later from the body. The calf moves very little at all at this time, a fact which is verified by the litter of shed white hair within a circle of six feet diameter.

Few things are as beautiful as the young seals at four weeks old, now resplendent in a new coat of short and polished blue. Each calf is worth studying in the varying pattern of its coat and I like to creep up to these fat and sleepy little people. I put the back of my fingers against the smooth skin of back and belly and the touch is cool; then I touch lightly those exquisite little hands and they are warm. The animal heat of the seal is insulated and conserved by the blubber which now covers the body. Only the hands are lean and from them heat ebbs.

PLATE 19

MATERNAL CARE: AN ATLANTIC GREY SEAL COW AND NEWLY BORN CALF ON THE TRESHNISH ISLES

The seal calves have trebled their birth weight in four weeks and are now quite unlike the little babies we first knew. Weaning takes place at this age, the mothers go away, and the calves are left to find the ocean ways on their own. They are solitary little fellows who will play by themselves but not with the others. Social play is a later development. I found myself a little sad and wondering, looking down on that nursery at the south end of Lunga. A month before there had been fifty babies and a constant activity of mothers. Now, in these four short but crowded weeks, a charming infancy had gone. I had expected a longer period of parental education. The sea's edge means danger for the seal calves, but we see that infancy has become telescoped during the course of evolution and the period of danger is shortened. There is very little growth apparent in the young seals between the ages of one and nine months; it is as if they were stabilizing the gains made in that race with time and the mighty sea in early childhood.

The erosion platforms of the Treshnish Isles allow the seals to have their young near the water and the sheer ramparts of cliff prevent them coming far inland. But the completely rock-bound shores of Rona are at once harder and kinder to the seals. The animals do not normally have their calves near the water and the parents climb high and go far inland. It is not the sea, then, which is the great danger to these young calves, though the farther their parents come from the water's edge, the greater their possible danger. The adult seals have had a long and arduous climb from the sea on Rona and they stay ashore until the calves are reared. Thin and dirty they are by that time, all their beauty gone. And then they return to the mighty ocean where there is food and plenty and revivification.

The seal grounds of Rona provide one of the most wonderful spectacles of wild life in Britain or even in the world. The animals climb about the island to a height of nearly three hundred feet and the steep northern slope, which we are daily compelled to climb ourselves to fetch water, becomes a wet, muddy slide. Hundreds of babies are dotted about, and some of them are at the edge of sheer cliffs of a hundred to two hundred feet. Fianuis becomes a morass and by November all the northern end of Rona from the hill ridge presents a scene of stark desolation. And yet this black bareness is a mass of life and a preparation for the spring burgeoning. There are the busy turnstones and purple sandpipers, the ravening black-backed gulls tearing up the many carcasses of dead babies, and the live seal calves themselves wandering about finding the best way down to the sea. This heavy manuring and trampling of the ground makes it ready for the coming year's greenness of chickweed. Only a few late calves are left in December and some spent bulls which look mere wrecks of the grand creatures they were in August. It is time they were away and, to speak the truth, we were glad to leave ourselves. We had been on the island during the two waves of activity of birds and seals and now it was just a stark shape in deep winter.

VI

SANCTUARIES FOR WILD LIFE

IT is one of the paradoxical aspects of our national life that we should have the name of being lovers of animals and of the open air, and at the same time be without one wild-life reserve of a national character. There are sanctuaries here and there, but they are maintained by private individuals, by groups of people such as bird watchers, and occasionally by public bodies. These small reserves are of value, but they are not sufficient to maintain a varied and widespread fauna and flora throughout the country. And it is not sufficiently understood what administrative difficulties are in the way of private and semi-public efforts to preserve wild life.

I wish to outline a national policy of conservation in this essay and to put a point of view, and I shall also draw on personal experiences to show how hard it is for an individual, however enthusiastic, to make headway.

There are a few factors positively and actively detrimental to the preservation of wild life—rough shooters who will kill almost anything, but particularly geese, ducks, and wading birds; game preservers of the type which kills any and all birds of the hawk tribe, and such animals as badgers, weasels, martens, foxes, and hedgehogs without any thought of the consequences other than the magnitude of the stock of game preserved; men who call themselves oologists and have an insane quirk of character which prompts them to steal as many whole clutches as possible of the rarest British birds; and there is a section of the community least to be blamed, the roving bands of untaught small boys.

It will be as well to remember, also, the depredations which may be made in the name of science, for they are apt to pass unnoticed or be readily accepted as necessary.

Imagine the discovery of a new animal and the immediate and respectable interest of Science with a capital S—that abstract figure of the searcher after truth which the general mass of people associates with science. Indeed, there is little need to imagine such a discovery, for there is the recent example of the African peacock, a creature undreamt of until a year or two ago. Wanton destruction or exploitation of this bird will doubtless be checked, for the possibilities of rapid extinction are beginning to soak into the administrative mind, but the calls of science may be its undoing. How many museum authorities are there in the world who will consider themselves justified in obtaining a specimen, preferably more than one, male, female, and immature? I venture to say some hundreds. Then there are the zoological societies whose toll is not the number of animals appearing in the various parks, but the three- to fivefold number, those which are caught in the natural habitats and are doomed to die before they reach the stage of exhibition. There are other scientific needs to be fulfilled as well, such as those of the anatomist and physiologist. The African peacock cannot be numerous, and unless a wooden-headed science can restrain its inquisitive hand, the African peacock will persist only in an atmosphere of camphor and carbolic acid. The attribution of specific rank to the St. Kilda wren in the eighties of last century almost caused its extermination in the hunt for specimens. Happily that has been checked and the little bird survives in an island cleared of humanity.

I believe there is far too much destruction of living things in the name of biology. It is the duty of every research worker to refuse to justify his killings unthinkingly as being in the interests of science. He should ask in the quiet places of his own mind how far his desired results might be obtained by not killing, but by expending more time and trouble. Might the knowledge sought be gained incidentally in some other investigation or chance death, and not by killing *ad hoc*?

PLATE 20

a. KITTIWAKE

b. AT PLAY IN THE POOLS
An Atlantic Grey Seal calf at one week old

I am here on Rona at a time when the autumn migration of birds is at its height. It was suggested to me that I should have a gun to shoot birds I could not identify through my field-glasses, so that knowledge of distribution and migration might be increased. I have certainly missed some small birds of the warbler type because I could not examine their plumage closely, but I cannot help feeling that their continued existence is of greater importance than the accurate knowledge I might have supplied by shooting them. The little birds, therefore, have gone their way.

Biologists need to learn a respect for life just as much as any other section of the community. Respect for life is not squeamishness. It is the regard which says in effect that here is an individual born into the world, moving with a quality called life which once taken cannot be replaced. If I kill knowingly and cut short this individuality, what lasting good can I expect from the act?

A respect for life is an entirely different idea from the refusal to take life. We are inevitable killers, almost in every step we take, and if we did not actively continue to kill we should fail to survive ourselves, either individually or as a species. But consider killing one fly on a window pane. What good is that going to do? The positive act of squashing one fly can have no effect in lessening the future population of flies and it is doubtful if any immediate end is served except stopping the buzz. Such an act is little better than wanton and not as justifiable as burning a maggot-infested carcass.

Those of us who are prepared to accept the necessity for killing will not fail in our respect for life by being prepared to do the killing ourselves. There is something contemptuous in the person who will enjoy and comment on the succulence of a fattened chicken on the table, but would be horrified at the idea of pulling its neck in the poultry yard. I admit that everybody cannot do his own killing for food, but we might all well disturb our complacency occasionally by remembering that our delegation of killing to some one else is not the most pleasant thing to have done. When it is necessary to kill an animal for science, food, or self-defence, be it harmful insect, beautiful bird, or mammal, think well first, but when the act is before you emotion should be laid aside. Do not hate, love, gloat, nor regret; kill well and cleanly and be done with it.

I like to think of the example of Edward Wilson of the Antarctic in connexion with this subject, and the following quotation from Mr. George Seaver's *Edward Wilson: Nature Lover* is apt:

'It is worthy of remark that this man, whom love of nature made so sensitive to the sacredness and loveliness of all living things, could force himself in self-appointed duty to kill the things he loved; and refined as he was in tastes and feelings to the point of fastidiousness, could cheerfully immerse himself for days on end in a welter of blood and blubber.'

If we hold to this respect for life we shall not kill for sport. There are innumerable arguments in favour of sport, but none of them can counter the simple question of whether it is right to kill for fun. I do not believe polemics with sportsmen will cause them to alter their views, and I for one should never quarrel with a sportsman who shot the creatures I love. There exists a complete difference of outlook which will alter only by education of the young, by showing people the beauty of an animal's private life, and by perseverance towards one's own ideals. I restate the point that there can be no ethical justification in killing any living thing for fun, as a trial of skill or as a healthy exercise. This outlook is not one to be pushed down people's throats, but to be held faithfully in every situation by those who feel it. It is a view which will grow; I know this most surely from within.

There is a large number of factors which are indirectly or passively harmful to the survival of many kinds of wild life. Drainage of the fens exterminated the large copper butterfly more surely than the collectors. It must be realized that extension of husbandry in new countries, the increase of human population, forest clearance, and the prosecution of large public works of drainage are the major limiting factors to the maintenance of wild life. The destruction is not of the animals as individuals but of their habitats. There is also public apathy as an indirect factor. The great mass of inertia may not destroy willingly but it lets die, which is just as bad.

One serious direct threat on a world-wide scale is that of commercial exploitation of a wild-life resource to supply the whims of centres of population far removed from the location of the animals themselves. There is the marketing of various kinds of wild duck in America, the duck which migrate along well-defined 'fly-lines' in the States and are bred in the great lake-dotted areas of Canada. A most flagrant example is the establishment of fox farms in Northern Greenland because there are still a few herds of that rare animal the musk-ox remaining in that area. They are easily killed by modern methods and make a cheap source of food for the fox farms. Dogs drive the musk-oxen into the characteristic stationary ring-formation which they adopt in the face of danger, and the fox farmer has merely to shoot them at close quarters.

The wearing of expensive furs is another serious factor making for extermination of rare species. Those who wear them should remember that for every skin worn probably three or more animals have been killed, wastage occurring in the traps, in the effect on the family life of the animals, and losses in transit and preparation of the skins. The slaughter of whales and seals is another example of commercial greed overreaching itself. The only hope for such animals, unless international action is taken, is that their numbers should sink below the level of profitable hunting. The industry then dies and the small stock of animals remaining has a chance to increase.

Only occasionally does sport take on the destructive qualities of a commercial undertaking as, for example, in the organization of safaris in East Africa, and in the increasing tendency in Britain to run syndicate shoots on ground not owned by the contracting sportsmen. The criticism which is easiest to make of British sport is that an unnatural increase of game is aimed at and got by methods destructive to many forms of wild life which are of direct usefulness to the rest of the community.

It is interesting at the present time to wonder how far game preservation has helped or depressed the general level of wild life. With certain exceptions, and without subscribing in any way to a justification of field sports, I believe it to be an exaggeration to blame the sportsman for the disappearance of many species. He may be one of the most potent factors in preservation of some, and this is apparent in our own country. It is safe to say that the red deer and probably the roe would not exist to-day as wild animals in Britain were it not for the sportsman. I am also sorry to think that the fox would have disappeared from lowland districts were it not for the sport of hunting. Other forms are protected incidentally because the animal hunted must be given its habitat more or less intact. The quietness of a large area of deer forest where grouse and ptarmigan are of no consequence allows the golden eagle to persist and even increase slightly. A fox-hunting country must have a fair sprinkling of spinnies and coverts which are visited comparatively rarely by the earth stopper, and such a distribution of covert and scrub is of the greatest value to numerous species of small birds.

The admission of such a state of affairs is in no sense a reason for the continuance of sport, but I feel that sportsmen and those people naturally opposed to such pursuits have a common ground for co-operation, for surely we all wish to preserve and conserve the wild life still remaining in Great Britain.

The term *conservation* of wild life is comparatively new, being first used in this connotation in 1909 by Theodore Roosevelt, who was a champion of wild creatures in

America. The term is in general use in the United States and Canada, but it has not filtered through to British usage—perhaps because there has been no conservation! Before Roosevelt's time a few people had thought, rather ineffectually, about the protection of wild life; but now an impartial biological science is gradually offering facts and findings, and the time is coming when loss will depend on lack of action and goodwill rather than on lack of technique.

Nevertheless, our bulk of knowledge is not by any means adequate for the sure preservation of a representative wild fauna, and research is hampered to some extent because we have no large wild-life reserve where conservation studies can be conducted without disturbance. Such work as is being done by a comparatively small number of biologists is not being applied to actual conservation because the law is in an archaic state concerning the care of wild animals.

Here are some of the personal difficulties I have encountered in getting very small islands observed as sanctuaries. The grey lag-goose is one of our rarest breeding birds and the resident race of the Summer Isles has been reduced to a very small number. I have worked for two seasons on one of the islands, Eilean a' Chleirich, and because I have been there, the whole of the bird life has been safe from molestation ashore, and I have been able to note a distinct increase in numbers and variety of birds living there in the third season. The owner of the islands and the grazing tenant of Eilean a' Chleirich have been extremely sympathetic to protection of the geese and other birds, and the owner has now proclaimed the island as a complete sanctuary. All well and good, but when people who ought to know better come to the nearest crofting township to these uninhabited islands and offer a pound an egg for all the wild goose eggs that can be obtained, protection becomes difficult. There is redress in law certainly, but procedure is expensive and that gives the law-breaker immunity. The police do not take action as a matter of course; the action must be led and few of us have the money to lay the case and follow it through.

The freedom of the sea is another devastating loophole. Small parties of tourists armed with shotguns have come from the mainland in launches and shot at anything that flies from the island cliffs. These people sail slowly round the island and as the birds fly out they try their skill. Cormorants, shags, herring gulls, black guillemots, razor-bills, and rock doves are shot and left lying on the surface of the sea. And this takes place often enough in June and July when the birds are breeding. These species are not 'protected' by law, the cruelty of killing parent birds which have young at the nest is not 'criminal', and the shooters have not trespassed. Some of them have given me a friendly wave as they have steered away from the island.

There is another island of which I own a small part and the rest is owned by a man who is sympathetic to the idea of the whole island being a sanctuary. But the island has a sporting assessment made by the rating authority, and although the shooting is not let, the rate of more than half the assessed sporting rental must still be paid. The owner naturally wishes to get this back. Now if I pay him this rent in order to keep the island as a sanctuary and so that I can have the legal privilege of a sporting tenant with regard to poaching, I must pay half the sporting rates as well. The fact that my aim is to kill nothing does not call forth the sympathy of the county council. Indeed, if the owner of a Highland estate proclaims it to be a sanctuary, and thereafter there is no shooting, he will still have to pay the sporting rates, which are always high. We may take it that county councils would view with alarm any extension of the notion of protecting wild life! Imagine a Highland estate of 20,000 acres, the shooting of which is let for £250 a year; the owner will pay £65 in sporting rates *whether he lets it or not* and the possible tenant will pay another £65 rates. The owner has received £185

PLATE 21

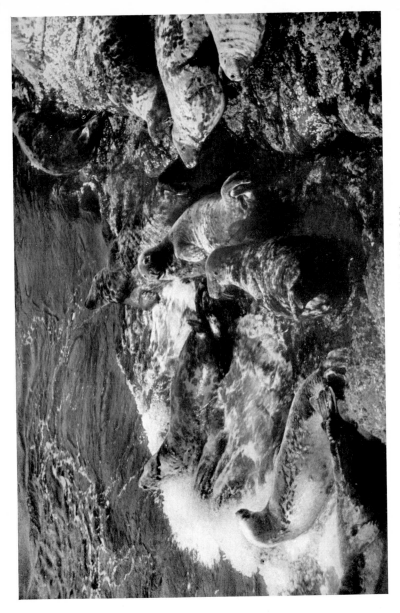

FLOWING TIDE: SEALS ON RONA

net, assuming the place is let, the tenant has paid £315 and the county council has got £130. An owner cannot afford to make his estate a wild-life reserve while this position continues.

Since I began this essay the subject of sporting rates on ground owned by the nation but not let for sporting purposes has arisen in the Courts, with a resulting decision unfavourable to the National Trust for Scotland. The case concerned the tract of one-time deer forest, recently purchased for the nation, bordering on Glencoe and including the mountains of Buachaille Etive Mor and Bidean nam Bian. The intention of the National Trust is that the area should be in effect a nature reserve, although that is not the immediate purpose. The value of this area as a deer forest pure and simple is now much diminished because of the free access given to these famous mountaineering peaks at any time of the year. Nevertheless, the deer remain, and if the area is to be properly managed by the National Trust, the poorer stags must be shot from time to time and a percentage of the hinds as well. This normal act of management took place and the Argyll County Rating Authority pleaded successfully that the ground was therefore liable to the sporting assessment which it had borne before it became Trust property. It is unfortunate, perhaps, that the chairman of the Trust took part in stalking these inferior stags. The case might not have been considered so clear if the beasts had been shot by the ranger staff as a routine duty.

If our wild life is to be actively conserved on a national basis there must be a change of attitude towards the laws already existing for the protection of some species. County councils paste up notices each spring announcing protection of a large number of birds listed under the Wild Birds Protection Act. The official function then appears to have been fulfilled, and those who wish continue to shoot rare birds. It is quite likely that when something particularly rare is shot, a paragraph will appear in the local paper describing the shooter's experiences. This happened fairly recently when a hoopoe was shot in the Beauly Firth. The shooter said he had been trying to get the bird every day for a week. There are still well-known egg collectors who can openly hold an exhibition of British birds' eggs, and as recently as June 1937 one of them had the show announced as an item of news in our premier scientific newspaper. There are animal protection laws, also, under which a prosecution has never been made, not because infringement has not taken place, but because it has been ignored or the law has not been backed up by means of preventing or proving infringement.

Wild-life conservation is a subject which can be influenced by so many factors; nothing is static, and many apparently unconnected actions have a habit of intertwining and producing obvious consequences. This very depth and quality of ramification in the subject makes it a difficult one to tackle administratively, and that is one of the main reasons for undertaking research into conservation methods at an early date.

I will give what is in part an imaginary, but none the less possible, example of the effect of politics on the survival of an animal species. While land is in private ownership certain creatures are fostered, others repressed, but broadly speaking there is evident a sense of responsibility and many forms of life have a better chance of survival than in a country where there is not direct ownership of the ground nor nominal responsibility for the wild life thereon. The deer forests of Scotland are privately owned and the deer belong to the owner whose ground they occupy at any one moment. The code of stalking is very strict in that an owner does not allow a bad shot to stalk at all; being an owner he usually has sense enough not to shoot the best-antlered stags, but to leave them for breeding; and lastly, if a stag is wounded, an unwritten law makes that sportsman follow up the animal and do everything in his power to finish it off. The result is that the percentage of cripples in Scottish forests is very low, certainly not more than one per cent. of the total kill.

Now in parts of America, where the game is state-owned, a hunter may take out a 'one-buck licence' and shoot his one head in any part of a large area of forest. It is estimated that the number of cripples in some parts of the deer grounds is as high as twenty to thirty per cent. of the total kill. It has been suggested from time to time that the Scottish deer forest ground should be nationalized and the sport thus thrown open to a much larger number of people. Personally, I do not think our small area of forest country and its deer would stand up to this type of syndicalization. The present owner stalks his forest scientifically and he is prepared to take the advice of his stalker, who is naturally careful to keep up the deer stock on the place. If there was no direct responsibility to be taken either by stalkers or by hunters, I feel quite sure that the percentage of cripples would rise and the best heads disappear. Think what would be happening really: the mature animals, including those with the best heads, are normally those which come first into rut, and the great bulk of the calf crop in the following year is sired by these stags. The very late calves are begotten by the young stags which run with the hinds when the main course of the rut is over. If, then, that very best group of the stag population is being depleted as much by crippling as by legitimate deaths, it will mean that a greater part of the calf crop will be born late. Late calves would be better not born at all, for the winter mortality rate among them is inordinately high. It will be seen that a population diminishing by such means is in serious danger of extinction, for apart from these obvious causes there are obscure psychological checks to increase in the herds. It would be foolish for me to say that nationalization of the Highlands will never come about, but if it does, some system of rigid reserves will have to be devised as a buffer against the changed human politics. I think, also, that with land ownership as it is we still need wild-life reserves as a check against extinction of certain species. My aim in describing two types of deer stalking has been to show that human politics, so often thought of as a subject for the arm-chair or the soap-box, can be a major ecological factor in the lives of animals.

The biological science most nearly concerned with wild-life conservation is that of ecology—the knowledge of animals in relation to their environments. It is the science which attempts to find causes and measure consequences, that it may be able to forecast consequences of the inter-actions of a known number of environmental factors.

You have often heard quoted that little ecological sequence of Darwin's—that the increase of the number of cats in a certain area increased the clover-seed crop, the steps being that the cats killed the field-mice which robbed the bees' nests which contained the bees which fertilized the flowers of the clover. That is ecology at its baldest, and chains of events do not always follow as simply as in the cat and clover story. Animal ecology is being pursued with vigour in this country at present. The group at Oxford is working particularly on the dynamics of animal populations. Our knowledge of fluctuations of numbers of certain species and of the factors bringing about these changes through a series of years is largely owing to the investigations conducted from Oxford. These workers have more recently done some extremely interesting work on the daily and nightly movements of small rodents, a subject about which we could do little but conjecture a short time ago.

Another branch of ecology, that of habitat studies, is typified by the work on Studland Heath, near Poole Harbour in Dorset. This work is naturally of immense importance in relation to wild-life conservation. The life of inland waters is now being studied from the Freshwater Biological Station at Wray Castle, Lake Windermere, and the life of the shallow seas is studied at the Marine Biological Stations at Plymouth, Lowestoft, Milport, and Aberdeen. At the same time we have no ecological field station as such, where workers could be trained and conservation studies made. Unfortunately, animal ecology takes but a small place in the biology courses in the universities.

My own work is on the borderland of ecology and the study of animal behaviour. What do we know of how wild creatures spend their lives? The literature of natural history is full of animal anecdotes, but there are comparatively few books giving a consecutive story of an animal's life. I am trying to find out what animals do and what are the factors influencing them in what they do. If we are sufficiently inquisitive, we can find out much of the effects of environment on behaviour, and such knowledge is of direct application to wild-life conservation. I have paid particular attention to the social behaviour of animals and I can now see that if human activities interfere markedly, though unwittingly, with the social systems of gregarious animals, very serious damage may be done to a stock without positively setting out to kill any animals at all. Animals often have territories on which they breed or feed, and you can imagine how easy it is for us to upset these. Some grazing mammals make an orbital movement which may take a year or even two years to complete; suppose some human activity such as the building of a fenced railway cuts right across that orbit: the pattern which may have taken countless years to become established cannot be completed. The animals may achieve some adaptation but, also, they may not, and their numbers may then be seriously depleted. I am finding, also, that if a social pattern in a species is not completed, breeding may not take place at all. There are some animals, of which the Atlantic grey seal is an excellent example, in which the social system may lay them open to extremely rapid decline in numbers if we do not protect them. The grey seals are not markedly gregarious during the first seven months of the year and nearly all their time is spent at sea. If crofters, fishermen, and sportsmen shot at them as hard as they liked for this period, as long as it was not in the immediate vicinity of the breeding-ground, I do not think the stock would be in any fear of extermination. But the grey seals have a very few sharply demarcated breeding-grounds to which they flock in August. The animals are ashore for a longer period than they are in the water in September and October, while the young are being born and reared, and if they become the object of sport (?) or commercial exploitation at that time, I am certain the whole species could be wiped out in a few years. This very nearly did happen in the late nineteenth century, when an increasing urban market for pelts made annual battues at the breeding-grounds a profitable business. Fortunately those days are over and this magnificent seal has increased in numbers. However, this peculiarity of its social system makes it incumbent upon us to provide at least one remote island which can be called a sanctuary for the grey seals. The animals are certainly protected by law for part of the breeding season, but we need a national sanctuary also as a complement to the law.

Law-making in the interests of wild life should take cognizance of the growing body of ecological work, but the greatest step forward will be when the State establishes wild-life reserves in the more remote parts of the country. They would serve the following public ends immediately: the wild life therein would be given breathing space for a time; the reserve would be a place in which the public could take pride and have healthy enjoyment; research into problems of conservation could be conducted with a scope and continuity of policy impossible at present.

The type of wild-life reserve I have in mind is an area of mountain country of 100,000 to 200,000 acres with a fair amount of shore line. This area would be zoned into absolute sanctuaries where the public would not be admitted without special permission, areas where possibly

PLATE 22

EILEAN A' CHLEIRICH

any reasonable person might be allowed to fish, and a third, outer zone where the public could move and act at will, as long as nothing positively detrimental was done to the interests of the animals of the reserve. This outer ring, which would be the part most commonly visited, would serve as a biological fence to the innermost sanctuary and would add to the holding power of that area.

There are two main ideas as to the type and function of a national park. One is that of a large area of country of varied scenery wherein humanity can walk and play undisturbed and in freedom. Rest-houses and camping sites are provided in such a park, and good motor roads are available. Such a park is a lung or playground for urban populations, and the particular area is preserved from unplanned exploitation. The Scottish National Forest Park which has recently been established at the head of Loch Long, within easy reach of Glasgow, exactly meets this need. An area in Skye, dominated by the Cuillin Hills, the Cairngorm region of the Central Highlands, and the northern half of Arran have become national playgrounds by invasion. There are many parts of the Highlands also where walkers and tourists enjoy reasonable freedom of access. Scotland is much better off in this respect than England and Wales.

The other conception of a national park is much more that of a wild-life reserve for our native fauna and flora, and that is the name I have given throughout this essay. Its needs are different from those of the type of park just described. Difficulty of access would be a direct advantage, for the provision of motor roads and camping sites would split up the territory and limit its value as a faunal area. The roughly concentric zoning of the reserve on the lines suggested would prevent the criticism that the public was being prevented from enjoying that which it was preserving. Another reason for the reserve being situated far from populated or agricultural districts would be that the animals of the reserve might be troublesome in adjoining areas, this especially if protection within the reserve had engendered a tameness and unusual boldness.

A national reserve should present such a variety of natural habitats as would include, attract, and maintain a representative section of our fauna and flora. The West Highlands would be peculiarly suitable, for within a limited area there are sea cliffs, sand-dunes, saltings, glens with deciduous woods, birch scrub, coniferous woods, deer grounds, and high tops. There are also plenty of freshwater lochs and rivers. An area in the Central Highlands, such as the Cairngorm region, would not be entirely suitable for a natural sanctuary because most of it is above a thousand feet high and there is no sea-coast. Obviously, most species of sea birds, many waders, and small birds would not be present in the Central Highland region. The West Highland area north of the Great Glen possesses many islands which are well on the way to being natural sanctuaries. Means should be provided for taking some of the public to these islands at a cheap rate, for to see and hear a cliff full of ledge-building birds is an experience which few enjoy, not least because of the expense in reaching such places by private hire.

It would be necessary in the early years of the reserve's existence to create natural habitats for certain animals, especially birds, in order to enrich the number of species present and to encourage greater numbers of some of the rarer ones. Shrubberies of indigenous berry-bearing plants may be planted or allowed to develop naturally, and there should be a progressive scheme of planting. The Highlands have been denuded of large areas of natural birch and pine woods during the last three hundred years, and it would be wholly advantageous to bring back rough, park-like woodlands within the reserve.

Another object of the reserve would be to encourage friendly relations between human visitors and the higher members of the fauna. It would be easy for the staff to rear a few individuals of several species of birds and mammals which, though living in freedom, would be tame and would help to establish a relationship of trust throughout the animal population of the reserve. It would not be unreasonable to hope for the rehabilitation of some animals now extinct in this country, such as the beaver, reindeer, and even wild boar. Possibly the public would frown on the enthusiasm which would reintroduce the bear and wolf!

It should be feasible to formulate an open scheme whereby owners of neighbouring estates and islands might co-operate with the national reserve in affording protection to some species which may be resident on their ground. In any case, it would be necessary to have the goodwill of the local landowners and the rest of the human population of the area.

There is also room for co-operation on a wider scale throughout the country. The large societies and bodies interested in conservation might co-ordinate their efforts; county councils and municipalities could easily establish all their parks, open spaces, and precincts of reservoirs as sanctuaries, and without much expense add to their attraction to birds. This policy would also add to their attraction for the public, and these places would become more of an amenity than they are at present. When the State reaches the point of spending money on wild-life conservation, I hope the many natural history societies who have established and maintained bird sanctuaries at their own expense will not be forgotten. Small subsidies to these bodies would be a most economical expenditure, for the labour and care are voluntary and gladly given.

Roosevelt's idea of 'conservation through wise use' does not mean blind preservation of everything. If some forms of wild life were looked upon as natural resources and drawn upon carefully, it seems probable that preservation would then be more sure. Both large and small reserves require a certain amount of human interference to maintain a biological rhythm with not too long a swing. There is danger in sentimentally giving sanctuary to all comers. Imagine a pleasant little marsh inhabited by grebes and waders which becomes invaded by an annually increasing stock of black-headed gulls: these last will almost certainly oust everything else and eventually alter the vegetative complex as well. The clear pools will become places of stinking green slime, and what was an all-the-year-round habitat for birds would become merely a seasonal one. The factor which usually keeps the black-heads in check by a toll on the eggs, man himself, must continue to do so.

We shall probably have to wait years for a changed convention, but the surest way to bring this about is through education of the young. It is not suggested that that well-known camel's back, the school curriculum, should be broken by the last straw of conservation taught as a subject, but in a school where conventions are very easily made and count for much, a regard for wild life could be very surely inculcated without actually teaching it.

When I look back through this essay I realize it is neither literature nor science, but rank propaganda! If you feel the urgency of the problem and dearly love the creatures concerned, perhaps you will forgive me.

VII

THE MYSTERY OF ANTLERS

THE lives of men and of deer have been inextricably mixed ever since there were men, and there can be little doubt that before the domestication of cattle and sheep man was one of the chief predatory animals affecting the herds of reindeer, red and fallow deer. Northern man tamed the reindeer, and though he is still in effect predatory upon them, he conserves them also and has evolved a culture wholly dependent on this animal, a culture which still survives among the Reindeer Lapps of Europe and many tribes of the Siberian coast.

The deer of temperate zones have lost their primary significance as a food supply in face of advancing civilization and the development of agriculture. They are now hunted in refined ways to afford sport to the few, and they may be kept in parks under almost tame conditions. But whether it is the woodland caribou of Newfoundland forests, the moose of Alaska, the reindeer of the Lapp, or the red deer of Britain, the antlers carried by these animals have never lost their interest or charm for those whose life is cast among them.

Our early ancestors were quick to catch at the idea of antlers as a symbol of adornment, and those furnishings themselves, whether cast naturally by the deer or taken from the dead head, were of immediate usefulness. Many prehistoric sites show signs of excavation by picks which were simply the antlers of deer. The brow tine was the working point, the butt or coronet the fulcrum, and the shaft of the antler was grasped as a handle.

It is remarkable how easily held is an antler in the human hand. There is an orderly succession and variety of curves and points which make the antler a natural tool, an extension of mind and eye, of arm and hand, to effect those innumerable actions of leverage which are characteristic of our very humanness. I have noticed in my own camps, when working in the forest, that I usually had a cast antler by me, especially as a fire tool; nothing is better for scraping the embers together or lifting a pot from the blaze. I was interested, also, to see how my son took a cast antler for his play and used it as a pick, and in other ways as a tool, when he was five years old, without prior suggestion from me.

Although superseded at a comparatively early stage of man's history, antlers must have been among his first tools, and perhaps he originally copied the natural twist of the antler in many of the tools which are in use to-day. The antler was no artefact, but a natural tool of which man very quickly took advantage. I look with regret on the fall of antlers from this dignity as a thing for work in the human hand to their present empty glory in hall or smoking-room, or to their final degradation as pegs for bowler hats.

The antlers of reindeer and fallow deer are palmate or flat near the points and the several square inches of smooth, white surface must have been an invitation to our early ancestors to draw upon it. And we know that they did scratch delicate and graphic pictures which are among the most indestructible examples of primitive art.

Man's preoccupation with these structures has nothing to do with the antlers in relation to the animal upon which they grow, for we shall not subscribe to the doctrine of the Swiss Family Robinson which might credit the Almighty with giving antlers to deer in order that Man (with a capital M) could make buttons and knife hafts the more readily. Let us consider them as part of the animal and as a problem for the inquisitive mind already primed with an ancient interest.

The outstanding fact about antlers is that they are not permanent structures on the heads of the Cervidae, the one family of mammals which grows them. The horns

PLATE 23

RED STAGS

which are characteristic of many of the ruminant mammals, to which group the deer also belong, are a product of the activity of the skin and are a modification of hair growth. They grow as the animal grows and remain with the beast throughout its lifetime. Horns are tough masses of keratin, an extremely durable compound of nitrogen. Antlers grow from the bone of the skull and are of the same substance as bone, a stable compound of calcium and phosphorus.

It seems strange that these extensions of the skeleton should not serve the deer as long as do the horns of cattle and antelopes, for they are biologically expensive to produce. Comparatively few soils contain an adequate supply of calcium, and particularly of phosphorus, and most of the areas where members of the deer tribe are now found in the wild state are rather poor in these elements. The red stag of semi-barren Highland forests grows his antlers anew each year, though less strongly, as does his better-fed cousin in an English park or German wooded forest.

Nevertheless, the supply of phosphorus in the soil may possibly be a limiting factor in the distribution of the deer family. The soils of the continent of Africa are notoriously poor in phosphorus and no deer are found in Africa other than the Barbary stag in the north. This is a poor little beast at best, a degenerate sub-species of the red deer which has such a wide distribution over the palaeo-arctic region. There is no geographical reason why deer should not be more generally found in Africa, for at an earlier time there was a continuous land passage from Spain, a country in which, even at the present time, there are large numbers of wild red deer.

Antlers appear during the first year of life, the young stag or fallow buck growing small points which are not unlike small antelope horns when seen from a distance; but each year, until the beast is ten or twelve years old, the new set of antlers becomes more elaborate in the number of points, in shape, and in size. Thereafter, as the animal approaches senility, the antlers grow a smaller number of points, become less in weight, and show less symmetry of curve. The bodily condition of the stag is still further reflected in the antlers which grow in the year following an injury, when the antler on the *opposite* side to that of the injury is reduced in size and malformed in more or less direct relation to the seriousness of the hurt. It is not easy to understand this close correspondence between injury and the growth of one antler only, but given the fact, the change in side is an obvious consequence of the lateral bundles of nerves crossing over at the base of the skull before passing into the brain proper.

These bony structures that are such an expense to the constitution of the animal which grows them are not of service to him for all of the year, in so far as he uses them at all. Let us take April 1st as an average date when the antlers are cast by the red deer of the Highlands, and from them trace the development of the new set.

There are two patches to be seen at first which are, in effect, the wounds from which the old antlers have fallen. Healing is very rapid and a new velvety skin covers these areas within a day or two. A change can be noticed in these small centres of activity each day after that. The flat patches become convex, they bulge upwards and become almost globular, and then the soft and tender bulbs themselves appear to proliferate until the stag looks as if he had three carbuncles at the place where each antler should be. The skin covering these new growths becomes more velvety in texture and the bulbs lengthen into thick stalks. The scheme of the antlers is here in promise.

A thing which takes months to grow does not often convey the full beauty of the dynamic movement of growth to the human eye. Nobody, we may be sure, has seen the beauty of antlers developing as a single, con-secutive movement, though it can be imagined.

It is a matter for regret that we cannot adapt that wonderful technique of the Canti process in cine-photo-

graphy by which, for example, an opening flower is photo-
graphed once every few seconds or whatever interval of
time is decided upon. When the finished film is passed
through the projector at normal speed, the opening of the
flower has been quickened to a movement our eyes and
mind can follow. I shall never forget the similarity
between the movements of a happy child dancing forth
to meet the sun and, seen on the screen, of a drooping
aquilegia waking in the morning, raising its flower head,
and throwing back its petals to the light as if they were
wide-flung arms. And so would the growth of a good head
of antlers be beautiful to see as an unfolding and outpour-
ing from those convex buttons of skin on the brows of
the stag.

The growth of the antlers in size is complete by about
the end of July, four months after it began, and the head
of the stag at this time has a charm which is lost soon
afterwards. He displays as yet none of that rugged,
aggressive masculinity which is characteristic of the stag
in October. His neck is still slender and devoid of mane,
and he has that summer redness of coat unblackened by
wallowing in the peat. His eyes are mild and full, for his
life now is a time of gentle grazing and restfulness in the
high corries in the company of his fellows. The antlers
themselves appear larger than they are in reality, for the
'velvet' covers them to a thickness of at least an eighth of
an inch. The velvet also refracts the light and makes the
antlers alone a study of light and shade. The stag carries
his elaborate head-dress with an extreme care which we
are apt wrongly to interpret as dignity. But the impression
of dignity is certainly present in his comportment at this
time. The latent strength is veiled.

This beautiful velvety covering of the antlers is not
merely a slight protection to them during growth; it is the
means by which they are fed as well. The velvet is rich
in blood-vessels so that there is a very active and thorough
circulation of blood carrying the nutrient calcium and

phosphorus, organically compounded and in suspension, to the receptive structure of the new antler.

It is easy enough to state the plain facts of what occurs when the antler is full grown and the velvet becomes superfluous. That part of the antler nearest the head grows more luxuriantly on its circumference and a beaded ring of bony tissue is formed, known as the coronet. The blood-vessels which have passed upwards between the beads of this circlet become constricted as it grows and hardens, and the temporary arteries are ultimately completely closed. But we do not know fully the physiological basis of this regulation and, as will be seen later, diversion of energy.

The velvet, now deprived of its functions and of its blood-supply, quickly dies. There is only one end to dead tissue on the living body—to be sloughed off; and the stag takes an active part in removing the dead velvet. Very soon the antlers are festooned with hanging strips of decaying skin which may be rubbed off against trees, or against stones if done gently, and sometimes the stag gets the end of a streamer into his mouth and may chew at it until it is torn away from the antler. This dead and occasionally stinking skin is yet rich in those elements it brought to the antlers when it was alive, and many stags do not let it lie but will eat it. This practice is common in Highland forests where, as has been stated already, lime and phosphorus are hard to come by.

The same fate befell the old antlers which were cast in the spring. Almost immediately the stags began to chew them, working from points to butt, and in a few weeks time only the coronets and the inch or two of shaft above them littered the hill-side. It is not uncommon to see a hind chewing the points of a stag's antlers while they are still attached to his brow. This craving for calcium phosphate sometimes takes more extreme forms of being satisfied than that in which the animal chews its own antlers and velvet. Many stalkers have seen stags chewing the carcasses of rabbits, and in one hard March when thousands of frogs, tempted to breeding behaviour by an earlier mild spell, were frozen to death, I saw the stags eating them in the shallow pools where the poor creatures lay. The deer also eat up the whitened bones of their fellows dead a season before. I know a stalker who left his bone-handled gralloching knife in the hill, stuck in the ground haft upwards; when he went to fetch it the following day, much of the bone had gone from it.

It is interesting to set down the way in which these grazing animals, whether deer, sheep, or cattle, eat bony material or some unnatural food from which they may obtain calcium phosphate. Their behaviour is always the same. The antler or bone is taken between the hard, toothless pad of the upper jaw and the incisors of the lower. The lower jaw passes from side to side, giving the object chewed a half rotation to and fro. What is perhaps most interesting is the curious expression on the face of the animal while the chewing is in progress. The neck is stretched forward and the muzzle held forward and upward; the eyes are half closed. Across and across goes the jaw and the shuttle of bone for an hour or more at a time. The animal seems entirely abstracted and devoid of that liveliness which is evident when grazing is in progress.

During the four months the antlers have been growing they have been nothing short of a liability to the stag they adorn. They have taxed his constitution at the end of the winter when he was least in the condition to bear the strain. Indeed, the season of April and early May is the time when many deer of both sexes die, but there is an undoubtedly higher mortality among the stags than among the hinds. It is the common experience to find the population of deer in a given area composed of females to males in the proportion of two to one, though among the calf crop the ratio is almost equal, or, if anything, in favour of the males. This differential mortality may be taken as characteristic, and the burden of antler growth is almost certainly one of the causes.

Dr. Julian Huxley has calculated from a large number of data that antlers tend to become heavier in proportion as body-weight increases, and that in red deer the antlers constitute from 2·5 to 4·5 per cent. of the total body-weight. The extinct Irish Elk was nearly seven feet high at the shoulder and his antlers weighed almost three-quarters of a hundredweight. The leaner period which undoubtedly followed the richness of the Pleistocene Age would go hard indeed with a beast which grew that weight of antler each year in the summer period. Of the Irish Elk it may be truthfully said that the antlers ran away with the species. The red deer of the Highlands has saved itself as a species by a reduction of both body and antler size. The reduction has been not merely environmental but genetic as well.

The stag is exceptionally careful of his antlers while they are in velvet. An untoward injury to them at this time causes him great distress and he loses much blood. As in every association of individuals, small differences of opinion are common among the companies of stags. Antlers are rarely used on these occasions during the greater part of the year, and never during the period of their growth. Instead, the stags settle these momentary quarrels by rising on their hind legs and boxing each other with the fore-feet in the same way as the hinds do. But they do not fight in this way for long and they are not nearly so proficient as the hinds. Plate 22 records one of these amusing moments in the life of the deer forest and is typical in the attitudes of the standing stags and of those which are watching with apparent interest.

The stags with antlers in velvet are at a further disadvantage when the midges and blood-sucking flies become numerous. In Scotland the deer cope with these pests by going high into the hill where there is usually too much breeze for midges and the conditions are not damp enough

PLATE 24

RED STAGS IN VELVET

The stags use their fore-feet in quarrelling when the antlers are soft

for the blood-suckers. The reindeer of the Arctic coastal plains have no high hills near at hand where they can find sanctuary. Our red deer, by climbing three thousand feet in three miles, achieve an effective migration which may take the reindeer some hundreds of miles to equal. They go to the coastal peninsulas and islands and by various social efforts keep away the worst of the fly attacks.

One method which they employ is that of 'yarding'; the reindeer mass together in as open a place as they can find and the ground is trodden up with their excreta to form a mud which gives off the pungent odour of ammonia. All the same, the midges frequently attack the vascular skin of the velvet to such an extent that the antlers are ultimately mis-shapen. The distress endured by the deer is so great that their bodily condition falls away considerably at these times. Reindeer are the only members of the Cervidae which carry antlers in both sexes, so it will be readily understood that attacks on the antlers by flies affect the life of the whole herd, not merely the males which, being free of parental duties, might best be able to bear them.

It is well known that there is a very close relation between antler growth and the gonads—testes and ovaries. In red, fallow, and roe deer, where only the males carry antlers, the physiological relation is concerned with the testes, but in reindeer the interrelation is concerned with the ovary as well.

The whole subject can be more clearly understood by remembering first of all that the gonads not only produce sperms and eggs but sex hormone as well, for they are members of that important group of organs in the body known as ductless glands. This sex hormone, male or female, goes directly from the gonad into the blood-stream and has a variety of functions, one of which is the maintenance of the secondary sexual characters of the animal. If the male is deprived of an adequate supply of this hormone his bodily type, and to a certain extent his behaviour, lapses towards that of the female. The cock ceases to crow and his feathering becomes hen-like; the stag does not develop his mane, his voice, or the characteristic male shape. But the most obvious of all these changes are seen in the antlers.

A stag castrated when he has just cast his antlers in April will never grow them again. If the antlers are well grown but still in velvet when castration takes place, they remain in velvet throughout the year until the next shedding season, when they are usually shed, but have been known to be retained. Antlers which are clear of velvet may be shed a few weeks after castration or be retained until the next normal shedding season.

The castration of male reindeer produces similar results, though in this species the normal shedding and growth periods are quite different from those of the red deer, and the males and females follow different rhythms. As fawns, both sexes shed their tiny antlers about April 15th and the new ones are ready to peel off the velvet from the end of July onwards. This is essentially the same period of growth found in the red stag, but the adult reindeer buck sheds his antlers shortly after the rutting season, which lasts from the end of August to October. The new ones do not begin to grow until the following spring and are ready to peel the velvet at the end of July. If the reindeer buck were to begin growing his antlers anew immediately after the old ones were shed he would suffer from frost-bite very severely during the winter. It seems strange, however, that his antlers should not be retained through the winter as a possible defence against carnivorous enemies. The palmate brow tines, also, would be useful for digging in the snow as, indeed, they are used by the females.

The fact of the reindeer buck losing his antlers in the fall, when they have been complete and hard on his head for only three months, should prevent us from thinking of biological structures merely in terms of what use they

THE MYSTERY OF ANTLERS

are going to be. The attitude which should be taken in any contemplation of this kind is what has *caused* a certain state of affairs, not why it should be or what end does it serve.

Female reindeer retain their antlers throughout the winter and use them as weapons of defence and as spades for digging through snow to the moss beneath. Once more the linkage of antler growth with the reproductive cycle is evident; the reindeer doe sheds her antlers two or three weeks after the birth of her fawn, that is, a little later than the young or barren females. Should the doe calve out of season the antlers will be shed correspondingly. Arguments may rightly be from causes and not from effects, but we cannot help noting that the mother reindeer is fortunate in the retention of her antlers as possible weapons for a little longer at the time when her calf is born and is a helpless little thing for some days.

It will be well now to revert to further consideration of the red stag which we left at the stage of peeling the velvet from his new antlers. This process is complete some time in August, and by the end of the month the antlers themselves are no longer the pale colour of bone but dark brown with white and shining points.

His outward appearance begins to change from that character of mild and well-fed peacefulness which has been remarked upon already. The mane grows and the stag's neck thickens perceptibly. Those facial glands below the eyes which are inactive for most of the year now secrete an odorous yellow mucus which trickles down the face. It is not long before the companies of stags open the peat wallows which have lain unused since April and May. The animals move about much more and now, if there are any differences of opinion between the stags, the antlers are flourished and may be used to give the other fellow a quick dig in the ribs. Increased movement and a certain latent excitement in the herd is not conducive to a big paunch and further accumulation of fat. The stags are, in fact, eating less, and their bellies become small, so that by the middle of September they are brave-looking fellows, all front as it were, but in those small hind-quarters is the strength which will give the force to that thick neck and to the challenging antlers. Quarrelsomeness is more common in the herds, and between September 12th and 20th each stag goes away on his own, a wild fellow, black from his wallowing and ready to challenge others.

This profound change has occurred in the short space of six weeks, and there can be little doubt that the energy which went to antler growth has been deflected to produce the condition of the stag in rut. The interrelation of antlers and the reproductive system is evident once more. But the gonads, the testes in this instance, do not control their own function as ductless glands bringing about the rut. Their action is initiated and influenced by another ductless gland at the base of the brain, the anterior pituitary body. It is only very recently that it has been learnt how the anterior pituitary body acts as a central control on the other ductless glands of the body. Its switchboard mechanism, which is obviously displayed in antler growth and the sexual cycle of deer, is almost unknown as yet.

Antlers are least of a puzzle to us when the stag is in rut from the middle of September to the end of October, but they still do present us with problems not easily solved. Here is our dark-coated stag trotting forth to the hind grounds to acquire a harem for himself. If he is one of the earliest stags in rut he may have a whole herd of hinds without opposition, but ultimately he will be challenged and will lose all but a few of them, or at least the hinds will stray to other stags and he will be unable to keep them for himself.

Two challenging stags come within a few yards of each other with some real or imaginary boundary between them, such as a burn or a deer track. They bellow at each other, and if they come still nearer heads are lowered and antlers presented. If they fight now the stags fence delicately with their antlers for a little while before the serious lunge forward. Each stag tries to catch the other broadside on and not to be thus caught himself. The fight, therefore, is often little more than a shoving match, continuing until one is tired and runs away. Fights of long duration with serious results to either beast are rare.

This is a point worthy of emphasis, that fighting is not the common and perpetual affair which many writers of popular natural history describe as part and parcel of the rutting season in the deer forests. The stags are often content with walking up and down the boundary of their temporary territories and roaring at each other. When two of them have adjacent harems, this course may be said to be the usual one.

Another fact of exceptional interest in the encounters between stags is that fighting does not take place unless the combatants are fairly evenly matched, and the matching applies particularly to their equipment of antlers. There is the fact, but I cannot explain it. Two human boxers contest with each other having an intimate knowledge of their own weight and reach, which are important points in their chances of success, but are not part of their skill in fighting. It is improbable that animals have a very strong conception of self, and it is even less likely that a stag is aware of the design of his own antlers. I think there is no doubt, however, that he is able to take stock in his own way of his opponent's furnishings. When stags of unequal merit meet, the one of lesser ability turns tail and lives to fight another day.

It has been suggested repeatedly in this essay that antlers are more of a handicap than an advantage to the stag, and as far as his combative relations with his fellows are concerned, the theory is still further strengthened when the behaviour and success of 'hummel' and 'switch-horned' stags are considered. A hummel stag is one which never grows antlers. For him there is no exhausting period of antler growth in those early days after the winter. He can go straight ahead with the task of building up muscle and fat, and it is generally accepted that a hummel attains good condition earlier than antlered stags. And he is usually among those which come early into rutting condition. His ability as a fighter is well known to the stalker; the impact of a hummel's poll in the ribs of a stag seems to take far more out of him than the sharp jab of antlers. These polled stags are frequently masters of harems, though it is the opinion of many that hummels do not stay long in any one place, but are inclined to move away from a harem of hinds without being expelled by a fresh stag.

A switch-horned stag is one which has no points on his antlers other than the terminal ones and possibly the brow tines. I know from my own experience that such beasts are able fighters and usually keep their harems for a good portion of the rutting season.

It may be justifiably suggested that the antlers of a stag have a value as a weapon of defence as well as of attack, and if this is admitted, antlers bearing a large number of projecting points would be more serviceable than a switch-horned pair. There is no doubt that a stag can use his antlers very effectively against wolves or dogs, but taking a wide view of the subject we should remember that the hinds, which are the protectors of the young, have no antlers; and we have seen already that the reindeer buck casts his antlers shortly after the rut, to be without these weapons of defence during the winter and spring when the attacks from wolves are most likely to occur. It would be sounder reasoning to consider them as essentially bound up with the sexual cycle.

With all their disadvantages to the animals which bear them, how can we fit them into the scheme of natural selection, assuming that we admit this as a mode of evolution? Dr. Julian Huxley, from his statistical studies of body-weights and antler-weights of several species of deer, has suggested that in the course of evolution antlers may have increased in size and branching with increase in the size of the deer as a species, and, accepting the evolutionary value of an increase in body size, the elaboration of antlers would not require to be of an adaptive quality in order to be controlled by natural selection. They may be merely a by-product of increase in body size.

There is one more advantage which antlers may give, as much to the species as to the individual. I have remarked on the small amount of fighting which takes place, even in the rutting season; if each stag appraises the other's antlers, it is probable and possible that this display of natural armaments is sufficient to prevent actual fighting. Deaths and damage through fighting, within the species, constitute biological wastage, and any means which prevents waste must be given its credit. The feeling remains, nevertheless, that antlers, like other armaments, are an expensive form of bluff.

The biological riddle of their evolution, growth, and function cannot be said to have been answered yet.

VIII

FOREST AND ISLAND

ONE of the keenest joys of living is the experience of contrast in situation. I write this essay after a sudden and deplorable break in the period of six months on North Rona, caused by the international crisis of the end of September 1938. It was the last day of the month and I was in the middle of my work on the seals.

A ship appeared off the east side of the island, much to our consternation, because she was unexpected. We started the engine of our wireless set and received messages from the ship; we were to be taken off. I took to the hillside with a number of towels and spelt out messages in reply. Could we not stay? As the sea was too rough to lower a boat from the ship, would that not be excuse enough? No; orders were for us to be lifted.

The ship went away because she was unable to lower a boat, and we breathed freely again. But not for long. The immense swell beating on the western cliffs of Rona began to slacken, and the fresh wind from the east was not enough to make our leaving impossible, though it was difficult. The ship came back again soon after midday and the boat was lowered. We came away from Rona almost as we stood and it was not easy getting down the cliff to the heaving launch.

Three months on North Rona so far, and twenty-one months of the past two and a half years spent on small, uninhabited islands; not as research workers pure and simple, but as a family trying to live a family life. We had almost evolved a culture; certainly we had acquired a technique for living our isolated lives and the environmental complex of the islands had entered deep into us. It was the mainland and a stone house which would be strange. Here was no departure thought about and pre-

PLATE 25

THE GLEN, DUNDONNELL

pared for; we were lifted from one life and dropped into another; the intervening period was one of a few hours only on board a friendly little ship, and the contrasts were not dulled by travel through ports and on trains. From remote island in the North Atlantic to the deep deer forest country we came, in the space of a night.

The dominating factors in our life alone on the tiny islands are the sea and that which causes the state of the sea, the wind. The mighty ocean; how often does the Gael of the coasts speak of the sea in this way! It is no striving after effect or attempt at hyperbole, this constant allusion to the immense and unknown power of the sea. One day on Eilean a' Chleirich two years earlier almost to the day, we had found ourselves short of food because our relief boat had not called. The weather was calm and I had paddled over the eight miles of open sea to the mainland in my kayak. I was looked at askance by the people of the crofts as I lifted the little boat ashore.

'You will not be going back,' they said.

'I must; I have come for food.'

'But between here and Clerach is the mighty ocean. What will it be doing before you get back?'

It was a simple usage of common words—the mighty ocean. Calm it was, but before I got back over those eight miles that day the north wind sprang up and I felt in cold fright my own frailty in this immense turbulence.

These are days of human conceit in *conquest* of nature instead of feeling we are working in concert with her. But in my own mind I remain with those few old men of the Outer Isles who still go to where they can see the ocean as soon as they have risen from their beds. It is the first act of the day, this looking at the sea, and they take off their caps before this manifestation of their God. To us of the little islands the march of conquest means little; we are part of nature, small living things, and our philosophy of acceptance remains. Surely it is better to understand and accept the ways of earth and ocean than to lift

one's self out of the natural order and alternately fear
nature through ignorance or oppress her through knowledge as Western civilization has done.

We are forty-five miles from land on North Rona, and
as there is no harbour or beach the sea firmly sets a bound
to the feet. Only the mind can wander, and that it does
with a vividness of imagination not commonly felt in a
place throng with the affairs of men. Our hut is placed
in the tiny sheep fank at the narrowest part of the northern
peninsula of Fianuis. The distance is a hundred and forty
yards between the sea to the west and east, and we cannot
get away from the sound of it. That sound has great
variety, and we know what is happening out there when
we are in our beds and out of sight of the ocean.

One of the deep sea caves of the west side comes in far
enough to reach underneath the fank. The murmur rises
through the intervening rock and comes to our ears as we
lie close to the floor. We recognize a small sea of light
wind from the west; there is the growing rumble as a
disturbance afar in the Atlantic reaches the island as
a deep swell. The rhythm is regular and the beat long,
interspersed by the breaking surf. It is a noble sound and
a little frightening, but it carries no element of danger in
fact to us. A deep swell on the cliffs will not take the hut
away. Then a fresh wind from any northern airt will make
the sea splash without any great boom, and our mind's eye
gives a vision of falling spray as we hear it washing the
cliffs outside. A small wind from the east makes a constant rustling of water like a breeze passing through leafy
trees. It is incessant, rather pleasant, and without rhythm
or beat.

When a storm is raging the sea is hardly to be heard in
the greater sound of wind. A gale of wind always puts
some fear into us though we come through most of them
without damage. We have had tents on some of our
expeditions and a period of high wind is very wearing to
the nerves. A child in an adjoining tent is a source of

constant anxiety, for his voice could not be heard in the
screech of tempest. Such anxiety is groundless ninety-
nine times out of a hundred, but there is always that odd
chance. Children have a gift of sleep beyond ours. Time
after time either my wife or I have crept out in the night
to see if the boy was all right and to tighten the guy ropes
of his tent. He has always been sound asleep and uncon-
scious of the din and lash of the storm. It has been
amazing but comforting.

Even in the hut on Rona a gale is not to be despised.
We are open to the west and north and those airts might
be the most serious, but the fank is some protection and
we have built the dyke higher to reach the eaves of the hut
which is anchored with wire and boulders. This shelter
is good and because the wind reaches us without obstacles
it is steady.

The hill ridge of Rona is between us and the south-
west and forms a bulwark to save us from those dreadful,
raking gales of wind and rain which come out of the
Atlantic. But a hill is not the best of windbreaks, for the
baffled wind gathers somewhere near the top and comes
down with a terrific buffet. The hut shakes visibly, and
tired though we are and falling asleep between whiles,
these dunts of tortured air wake us suddenly again every
time. It is these buffets which are most critical for a tent,
for the force may be great enough to snatch the guys out
of the ground or rip the canvas.

Each of us is listening privately. Perhaps on the third
night when there seems no slackening there come occasional
seconds, no longer than a second each time, when there
is no wind. These are moments we have listened for each
night; they are the beginning of the end. Wonderful
seconds of silence, one in a quarter of an hour, one in ten
minutes, one in five—and the gale as strong as ever in
between. Where do they come from, these glorious
seconds? How can they be at all in a fluid mass of air?
Are they like bubbles in running water? The thoughts

flit through our minds and one of us after a while will quietly ask, 'Did you hear that?' When all is noise and tumult these moments of silence are heard. The seconds string together into minutes as the night is swept away and the storm dies.

One of the most wonderful experiences we have on the islands comes from the single days of idyllic calm and beauty which will follow periods of storm. One perfect day when the whole organism cries out for time to stop. Its healing power is very real. The Gael of the Isles knows it well, for he calls this day 'peace in the mouth of the beast'.

We are lazy ourselves on such days and take our meals outside. The animal life is lazy also, for the birds float quietly on the blue mirror of the sea, seals lie out for long periods on the warm rocks and forget to quarrel, and from the cliffs of Eilean a' Chleirich it was on such days we most often saw the otters playing happily in the sea. Our hens would wander far afield and the goats lie flat on their sides, legs outstretched and eyes closed. These days come on the Highland mainland also and they are enjoyable in the forest, but it is only on the islands that they have the ecstatic quality of peace and beauty. Was the storm real, we ask ourselves, can it ever be like that again? The still air is clear and there is no heat haze, and at such times I have lain on the summit of the cairn of Clerach, the Cruachan of Lunga, and the Tor of Rona and watched the silver scene the round of the compass.

Clerach: the eastern panorama of mountains from the Reay Deer Forest to Torridon, and to the west the length of the Outer Isles from the Butt of Lewis to North Uist. Lunga: Mull is to the east and her lovely outline culmin-ates in the peak of Ben More; southwards the Paps of Jura show above the dark Ross of Mull and the Isle of Iona gleams in the sun, for the white sands can be seen much farther away than where I am; the hills of Moidart on the mainland are to be seen to the north-east, and westwards from there is the blue, sharp outline of the Cuillins of Skye, then the peaks of Rhum, the dim line of Canna and Coll and Tiree nearer at hand. Through the sound between Coll and Tiree the Hebrides are clear, the light-surmounted battlement of Bernera at their southern tip and the twin cones of Hekla and Ben More in South Uist showing above the rocky outline of Coll. Rona: an immensity of ocean unbroken by the maze of little islands, and the far coast-line from Orkney along the North Coast of Scotland and down the west again till I can see the hills nearest me on Eilean a' Chleirich, which other home is but eighty-five miles due south. That far panorama of mountains is pale blue and remote in its beauty. The Butt of Lewis is rarely visible and the ocean remains unbroken to the eye till the rock of Sula Sgeir rises sheer, to the south-west by west, twelve and a half miles away. If I use a glass I can see the solans flying round the gannetry on pinions gleaming white. It is on these days on the little islands we reach apotheosis. The mighty ocean is between that far-off country we see and this tiny reality. Which is reality and which is dream? How often that question has flitted, half fancifully, half seriously, through the mind!

If we have lived a golden age it has been in the years of the little islands when the world of the mind has been of our own making. The great storms are not forgotten, but they are dim behind the abiding memory of good days. Those cloudless days of early March on Eilean a' Chleirich, when the frost is keen and the island quiet in its unwakened life; the wild barnacle geese are weak and do not fly much and some of them will come to feed with our hens; each evening we sit in the hut and watch the mural precipice of the island ridge of Torridonian sandstone. The wine-red rock catches the rays of a falling sun, to blaze forth vermilion until the darkening. Shadows are sharp, and the pillared, fluted rock throws an intricate pattern of little shadows as incisive as if it was engraved anew each night.

There are June days when the grass is lush about the lochans' edge and I take the goats to a fresh patch where a few dwarf willows are growing also. I watch those eager, selective lips taking the new herbage and listen to the teeth chewing it in a satisfying crunch. It is good to lie in the grass awhile with contented animals which like your company.

We have always found it difficult to go to bed in May, June, and July if the days are good. There is fishing to be done most nights, and as I sit on the boulders of the tiny inlet where the kayak is kept, I sometimes become conscious of what I am doing. The mind's eye seems outside of me and sees a barefoot man in tattered clothes opening mussels and baiting hooks, not for fun, but because he must win food for the family. On the other side of the island is a cave and a kitchen midden where man sat and prepared for the night's fishing thousands of years ago, just as he is doing now. Where is the Renaissance and its civilizing influence, where the rise of Science, and what has this man here to do with scientific research? He is just a man like a thousand generations of remote ancestors, gathering food from a giving earth and ocean.

We put the frail skin boat into the water as darkness gathers and paddle forth to skerries where the fish lurk. How thrilling the tugs on the line! I, who love the animals and profess to take care of them, find myself the early hunter. Only little fish get my pity and are returned to the sea, and when I have enough for ourselves and a boiling for the hens I have to discipline myself not to yield further to the thrill of the tugging line.

There have been other moments of this golden age, in the early darkening of November nights on Lunga of the Treshnish Isles, when we have stayed on the Cruachan to watch the deepening and fading of the sunset over the Atlantic. A quiet world but for the murmur of ocean and the clear crying of seals among the skerries. We would not change our lot for a path of comfort.

PLATE 26

SUMMER TASK: THE PEATS, EILEAN A' CHLEIRICH

The sky is an entity in the life of the island dweller as it is to the sailor. It was not until we came to Rona that I knew consciously the deep significance it had for us. We are usually out of sight of land and from the window of our hut is an unbroken expanse of sea to the east and north-east. The skies of Rona, whether it be day or evening, are the most magnificent I have ever known, and sometimes for hours together I have been content to watch their slow pageantry. Cumulus, cirrus, or nimbus, deep blue and white and rolling grey, pastel shades of pink and gold and green and violet—all pass the eastern horizon of Rona and bear constant watching because no dark line of land or mountain peak draws the attention of eye and mind. The windows of the island dweller should face eastwards or a little south of east, for most of the storms come from the western airts. The skies to the west are often threatening and disturbing, even when nothing bad does come. Eastern skies seem to keep that which was good until the last moment, and the sea on the eastern side does not constantly emphasize its immense power and strength. When that inexorable swell is pounding on the west and reaching into the caves below us, it is often resting to the mind to gaze on the less emotional sea and sky of the east. Stormy weather from the west does not look so bad when it is seen going away eastwards.

The mind does not stay familiar with sights and sounds of another world left far behind, or to put it in another way, the environmental complex of the islands is so full and vivid that we do not realize some of the common things of earth we have left, and which become rich experiences for our senses immediately on our return to the mainland. Here were we on the stark northern peninsula of Rona where much of the rock is bare and nothing grows higher than your feet; the sea was rustling eastwards and pounding to the west; the mother seals were crying a few yards away and as we woke that morning we were hearing the crying of a baby born only ten feet from

the door of the hut. Then the ship, the wrench and bustle
of our leaving, for me the misery of seasickness and an
hour of oblivion in sleep before waking to a calm Minch
and the sunrise over a sky-line I knew so well.

The hills of home came nearer and we passed under
Eilean a' Chleirich where a one-roomed hut stands always
ready for us, peats stacked under the lean-to, and food
lying in the cupboards and books on the shelves. It was
a temptation to ask to be set down there. We left the ship
off Cailleach Head and came ashore in a launch to the
crofting ground of Badluchrach on the south side of Little
Loch Broom. I leapt into the calm water and walked up
a shingle beach such as we had not seen for months; then
up the steep slope of the ancient fifty-foot beach which is
turned every year now with the *cas-chrom* or crooked spade.
I found myself in a clump of willows at least five feet high
and I thought it was the jungle itself for luxuriance. A
robin sang with flute-like clarity and I stopped to listen.
No bird *sings* on Rona; pipits cheep, and migrating flocks
of white wagtails and Greenland wheatears make a twitter-
ing and smatching; the other birds of the island have
raucous cries, but there is no song to compare with these
liquid notes of the robin.

On again now to a newly cleared patch of stubble where
straws snapped and complained beneath my feet. The
golden light of autumn was about and I stopped again to
let my nostrils enjoy the grand scent of new straw.
Associations crowded in on my mind and I knew myself
in a world of men after all where the earth was turned and
a harvest gathered. A strip of potatoes lay by the corn
stubble, the haulms dying now that the tubers were fat
in the ground. An old woman was bending low with a fork
on the outside row and I ran over to where she worked.

The old lady looked up at me without straightening.
Astonishment showed from the blue eyes set in a face
which had the beauty of a little wild apple.

'Is it yourself that's in it?' she cried, 'Isn't it on Rona you are now?'

But there was no doubt about it. There was I, smiling down at her, breathing in the noble scent of old earth newly turned and enjoying the sight of pink and white tatties peeping out of it.

Before I left the crofts there were still more common things to thrill me anew. I liked watching a horse moving and then I smelt the cows on the common grazing, that strange sweet smell of cows which is as the breath of domestication. Indeed, we had been out of the world of men; here it was, real and good once more, and it seemed immensely old. Here was true civilization, where men and women talked and did things for each other. Was it our island life now which was a dream?

We were soon at the little white house on the wooded brae face which is our home, and first of all a fire and a cup of tea. I ran outside to gather beech kindling, and we could have cried aloud with pleasure when the wood smoke came into our nostrils. The grate is smoky indeed and all our clothes are saturated with wood smoke, so much that people grin at us when we make a journey southwards and they get the strange scent from our clothes. At this moment we did not grumble at the blue smoke curling about the room.

I took a bucket to the burn for water. One of the things we miss most in our island world is running water and the sight and sound of it. Here in the forest there is no silence, for the burns are in every glen and gully, constantly fed by the high rainfall. When I had put the old copper kettle on the fire I went back to the burn to wash luxuriously in the clear unlimited water. Less than twenty-four hours ago we were using as little water as possible, for on Rona we had to carry it half a mile from over the hill, where the old well is at the edge of the cliffs on the south shore. Bad weather or good, we have never grumbled at having no water laid into our house. It remains a pleasure to run with a towel to the burn in the early mornings for the beauty of running water is never to be despised.

Nothing on the mainland is more beautiful to an island dweller than the growth of trees. Both my wife and I miss them, but we are agreed that if choice must be made between trees and sea, we must choose the nearness of the mighty ocean. This sounds a little fanciful in a modern world, but the hold of the sea and island shores is very strong and real and we are not ashamed to admit the feeling after these island years of our lives.

We take pleasure anew in the varying shape and movement of trees and in the shades of their greens. Each kind has a different rustle as the wind passes through it. The beech-trees run from our house to the burn and for a little way across. There, near our little fall and pool, is the grandest beech of them all. The trunk is short, immensely thick, and heavily gnarled in the way that fairies and tree creepers like. Thick branches strike out and as they ramify and grow thinner until the uttermost twigs are reached they make a parabolic curve. Beneath the beech-tree then is a brown carpet of leaves and plenty of open space below the green canopy. I stand there enjoying it afresh after Rona and bare rocks. Surely this beech-tree is a miraculous growth; its shade, and indeed the shade of any other tree, is more beautiful than the harsh shade thrown by a cliff or boulder. The sun glints through a myriad leaves which move their tiny ways in this gentlest of breezes. The spangled shade of trees is so common to people of the mainland that its beauty is probably never sufficiently sought after and enjoyed. It is a study in itself.

We had come from where the night was never quiet for the wild crying of the seals, and this night as we lay in our beds there was the constant sound of roaring stags across the glen. How many people can have been in such close contact with these animals, so widely dissimilar in themselves and in their habitats, in such a short time?

PLATE 27

DAILY TASK: DUNDONNELL

I was busy with axe and cross-cut on the following day
bringing in a store of birch and alder for long burning on
the fire, spruce for a quick blaze, and some hearty-burning
pine branches of middle thickness. A continuous wood
fire needs management and care in cutting the fuel. It
was good work, but an island's coasts were no longer setting a bound to my feet and I wanted to move and enjoy
more of the contrast of situation before my senses and
imagination dulled and accommodated themselves.

I went through the birch woods and then to the pine
woods where the roe deer are. These little elves of the
forest suited my mood, for their delicate features and
movements of ineffable grace were in such strong contrast
to the great seals ashore on the peninsula of Fianuis. I
saw them grazing towards me through the scattered clumps
of trees, feet raised high at each step and placed silently
on the ground again. The head poised on the flexible
neck and dipped into the herbage for small sprigs of moss
and heather; then it was raised erect with the large ears
outstretched while that sensitive muzzle tested the air.
The little white patch on the throat was plain, the rest of
the body seemed to fade into the darkness of the wood
and the eyes were luminous, large, soft, as only a roe's
eyes can be. They passed on silently as ever until I could
see only the pure white tail patches among the dim
columns of pine trunks.

My own feet seemed clumsy then as I climbed to the
limit of the trees. A stag was roaring up there and I
wanted to get near him. Fortune was with me this evening
because trees and weather hid my approach, and when I
dared to look about it was to see the stag with one hind
which was in season. The other deer were grazing away
out of sight behind a knoll, and these two were taken up
with their love-making enough to allow me a very close
stalk. I crawled flat through that wet ground to within
fifty yards and watched them through the brown stems
of the bents without the necessity of using a glass or

binoculars. It was grand; still only forty-eight hours from
Rona, the mighty ocean and the seals.

The hind moved with lightsome, ecstatic steps, raising
her muzzle to his and passing beneath his neck in an
abandon which excited him. He moved but little except
to take a step towards her each time she teased him. His
neck was heavily maned and dark from wallowing, and
every few moments he would raise and extend his muzzle
to roar. The sound was grand also at this short range,
especially so as my eyes were watching his wild eye and
open mouth. He would turn his head slowly this way and
that, and the beauty of spread antlers was heightened by
the very slowness of movement displaying them. Deer
are never more beautiful than in these moments of pre-
coital courtship. It is a phase of their life seldom seen by
man. I was back in my forest years again, alone and
seeking.

There is for me one striking difference between the life
of the forest and of the little islands; the social unit of the
family is much closer on the islands. I may watch the
birds or stalk the seals alone, but I am never more than
a mile away from the tent or hut which may be our home.
I go back there for food or my wife and son will bring it
to where I am and we eat together. Evenings are nearly
always spent together, and we set aside half an hour for
songs and the mouth organ, sitting by the child's bed.
The remoteness of a small family on a far island calls for
this expression of unity and good fellowship. But in the
forest I am alone and an individual. There I am a hunter
in effect, and a hunter must be alone and extremely
individualistic if he is to be successful. My food and gear
are in a little tent tucked away in some den or corrie. The
days are long and I may range far over rough country.
I neither whistle nor speak and for much of the time I
must not think, because my mind must be at the back of
my senses to receive what they find and tell of the move-

ment of the deer. When I return to my little tent at the darkening the day is not done, for I must cook and make a lot of tea to drink while I lie in my bag and think and write down the doings of the day. Perhaps I will go back to the little white house in the glen to-morrow, or perhaps in a few days' time, but until then I am a silent and self-sufficient individual, just one unobtrusive member of the mountain fauna.

The island is a pocket in the ocean with no land above a few hundred feet; here in the forest are mile upon mile of rough mountain, a changing scene of loch and corrie and swift-flowing river. I could travel a hundred miles and meet no fence. This is big country in every season; the island is small country set in the immensity of sea where my feet cannot tread.

PRINTED IN
GREAT BRITAIN
AT THE
UNIVERSITY PRESS
OXFORD
BY
JOHN JOHNSON
PRINTER
TO THE
UNIVERSITY